Brian Hill

Observations and Remarks in a Journey through Sicily and Calabria

Brian Hill

Observations and Remarks in a Journey through Sicily and Calabria

ISBN/EAN: 9783744762076

Printed in Europe, USA, Canada, Australia, Japan

Cover: Foto ©Andreas Hilbeck / pixelio.de

More available books at **www.hansebooks.com**

OBSERVATIONS
AND
REMARKS
IN A JOURNEY THROUGH
SICILY AND CALABRIA,
IN THE YEAR 1791:
WITH A
POSTSCRIPT,
CONTAINING
SOME ACCOUNT OF THE CEREMONIES OF THE LAST HOLY WEEK AT ROME,
AND OF
A SHORT EXCURSION TO TIVOLI.

BY THE REV. BRIAN HILL, A.M.
LATE OF QUEEN'S COLLEGE, OXFORD, AND CHAPLAIN
TO THE EARL OF LEVEN AND MELVILL.

FORSAN ET HÆC OLIM MEMINISSE JUVABIT.   VIRG.

LONDON:
PRINTED FOR JOHN STOCKDALE, PICCADILLY.
MDCCXCII.

TO

THOSE ORNAMENTS OF ANCIENT NOBILITY,

THE

EARL AND COUNTESS OF

LEVEN AND MELVILL,

WHOSE CONDUCT IN PRIVATE LIFE

ADDS LUSTRE TO THEIR RANK,

AND HONOR TO THEIR STATION,

AND WHO, WHILST THEY THEMSELVES SHEW FORTH

A PATTERN OF REAL PIETY

AND CONJUGAL FELICITY,

HAVE THE HAPPINESS OF SEEING A NUMEROUS OFFSPRING

WALKING IN THEIR STEPS,

AND IMITATING THEIR VIRTUES,

THE FOLLOWING PAGES ARE MOST

RESPECTFULLY DEDICATED, BY

THEIR MOST OBLIGED

AND MOST FAITHFUL

HUMBLE SERVANT,

BRIAN HILL.

PREFACE.

THE following pages were first put to paper with no other design than that of refreshing my own memory, and complying with the wishes of a few particular friends, who were anxious of hearing from me as often as I could find opportunity of writing to them. This made me take up the pen at almost every place where we stopped, and put down the occurrences of the day in order to furnish matter for my letters, which being usually written in the way of diary, will account for my frequently expressing myself in the present tense instead of the past, and plead my apology with the candid reader for whatever his judgment may discover as unfit for the public eye, before which nothing was further from my intention than to have suffered what I had hastily scribbled down as my first thoughts, and under every disadvantage of situation, &c. to have appeared. The real truth is, that having shewn my journal to a few intimates since my return to England, others wished to have a sight of it, and after them still more requested the perusal of the manuscript,

script, and very much urged the publication. I then refolved to print fome particular parts of my tour in our provincial newfpaper the Shrewfbury Chronicle, and to ftrike off a few copies for fuch of my own circle of acquaintance from whom I might expect a partiality and indulgence beyond what I was confcious the performance merited. But after I had actually fent it to the prefs, and it was announced by the printer for his next paper, I felt fo fenfible of the many imperfections of the piece, that I wrote to ftop its coming out, and told my friends what I had done; the confequence of which was, that inftead of being fatisfied with the fuppreffion of it, they were

were a great deal the more importunate for its being sent abroad into the world in form of a volume; and made me promise to comply with their solicitations. And thus have I acted in this business just like the poor wary clown who waded through a deep river for fear the bridge should not bear his weight. I know well that *the pressing request of friends* is the hacknied pretence of many a garretteer for obtruding his trash and falsehood upon the public; but if any thing in the following journal may be deemed the former, I can conscientiously assure the reader that I have steered perfectly clear of the latter, and not played off the traveller, instead of proving

proving myself the faithful narrator.

I AM not, however, without hopes that some information and amusement may both be gathered from the following sheets, to which I have made some additions, chiefly by way of notes, which were not in the original manuscript, and which, I flatter myself, will not be thought uninteresting; a circumstance which must plead my excuse for the length or frequency of the notes which may be interspersed throughout the work.

I cannot proceed any further in this preface without acknowledging the wonderful goodness of that Providence which so evidently presided

sided over us during the whole of our journey from Naples, till our return to that city, especially whilst we were passing through Calabria, a country, which though scarcely inferior to any other in climate and productions, and which for its sublime and magnificent views, forests of immense chesnuts, and stately oaks which flourish to the summits of the highest mountains, perhaps exceeds every other, yet affords for travellers no one convenience whatever; but on the contrary, they have every real danger and misery to encounter, and that in a much greater degree than in Sicily; especially from the gangs of banditti, which have considerably increased, and become

more

more desperate since the dreadful earthquake of 1783; insomuch that even the barons of the soil dare not move half a mile from their own habitations without being accompanied with armed guards.

When therefore I reflect that we have been mercifully preserved from these depredators and murderers, as well as that we have escaped in safety over precipices and mountains almost unexplored and inaccessible, through wide rapid rivers, where a single slip, either of our mules or guides, might have endangered our lives, and that during our stay in these volcanic countries there were no less than seven earthquakes, none
of

of which were felt by us, though two of them did confiderable damage a fhort while before we paffed the places where they were moft violent: I fay when I call to mind all thefe circumftances, and the unufual good health which was gracioufly vouchfafed to us when we ftood moft in need of it, I feel myfelf not a little thankful for the return of myfelf and friends to a land of peace, plenty, and comfort; a land over which the dark clouds of tyranny and oppreffion may not lower, but where the genial fun of freedom ever fhines, where every individual can fit without fear or difmay *under his own vine and under his own fig-tree,* and where every gift

gift of heaven, religious and civil, is the happy portion of its highly favored inhabitants.

Nothing now remains for me to add, but my sincere wishes, that if any of my countrymen, who may take the trouble of reading this work, shall think proper to visit either Sicily or Calabria, they may gather from it some hints which may prove useful to them in their tour, and some precautions which may tend to preserve them in safety

("Felix quem faciunt aliena pericula cautum,")

till they return to their native isle, to enjoy those constitutional blessings of *liberty and order*, under the benign

benign auspices of the BEST OF MONARCHS, which absence from it must only the more endear to them, and cause them to taste with double relish.

Harley-street,
Feb. 1792.

ERRATA.

Page 20. line 6. *for* 100 *read* 300.
—— 22. —- 1. *for* terminate *read* terminates.
—— 37. —- 2. *for* use *read* sale.
—— 49. —- 2. *for* infect *read* infest.
—— 52. —- 20. *for* lies *read* lie.
—— 62. —- 8. *for* from *read* form.
—— 119. —- 4. *for* dissolution *read* desolation.
—— 130. —- 1. *for* overthrown *read* overflowed.

☞ *The Binder is desired to place the* MAP *facing the Title.*

OBSERVATIONS AND REMARKS

IN A JOURNEY THROUGH

SICILY AND CALABRIA.

PALERMO, *February* 1, 1791.

WE set sail from Naples yesterday morning about nine o'clock in the Tartaro packet, commanded by Captain Chianchi, and after a very good passage of twenty-five hours, landed safely upon this island. As the distance is rather more than 180 miles, we thought ourselves extremely fortunate in concluding our voyage

voyage in so short a time, especially at a season when the weather in this climate, as well as in England, is very variable and tempestuous. The vessel is always furnished with provisions for twelve days, and being established by government, is well armed and manned to keep off the Turkish and Algerine pirates, who are always upon the watch to attack vessels of inferior force. The company on board formed as motley an assembly as was ever collected together; and would probably upon a longer acquaintance have afforded many curious and entertaining anecdotes. Besides the crew, which consisted of Italians and Sclavonians, there were two priests, a woman and child, three Englishmen, (viz. my brother Sir Richard Hill, my nephew and myself) an Irishman, a Welshman, a Frenchman, a German, a madman, and a murderer.

[margin note: burden]

The latter had fled to Naples, after killing a woman at this place, and was brought back in chains, to be delivered up into the hands of juſtice, which is much better adminiſtered here than at that city *. At the diſtance of twenty-four miles from Naples we ſailed under Caprea, a ſmall iſland, where the emperor Tiberius ſpent the laſt ten years of his life, in purſuing the moſt infamous pleaſures, and exerciſing the moſt wanton cruelties. It preſents an high ſhore, the north ſide of which is well cultivated, but the ſouth is only a range of vaſt naked rocks. 'Till we had paſſed this iſland the ſea continued ſmooth, ſo that we had full enjoyment of one of the fineſt proſpects imaginable. The city of Naples, large and handſomely

* Sir William Hamilton told us that the king of Naples loſes four, and ſometimes ſix thouſand ſubjects every year by aſſaſſinations. And yet there have been only two executions theſe twelve years.

built,

built, is all seen at one view. The shore extends itself on each side, so as to form a magnificent amphitheatrical bay, mountainous, but highly cultivated. On one side is Vesuvius, a great conical mountain, 100 feet higher than the famous Snowdon*, continually throwing out smoke, and, at the time of an eruption, flames twice its own height into the air: On the other side the hill of Pausylippo, ornamented with gardens, vineyards, and country houses; the Gulph of Baia, and the Promontory of Misenum, together with the lofty and fertile islands of Ischia and Procita.

Upon the approach of night, and just as we were losing sight of land, a rolling sea, which overthrew all the

---

* This mountain, which is the highest in Wales, is, according to Mr. Duten's calculation, 3555 feet above the level of the sea.

moveable

moveable furniture on board, forced me to my cabin, where I suffered so much from sickness, that I expected to become a victim to curiosity, and fully resolved never to venture upon sea again, when I could possibly avoid it. Early in the morning we passed under Uftica, which prolonged the misery of myself and companions (who were also very ill) a few hours, as the captain was afraid of coming upon that island before day-break.

As soon as I had power to rise from my hammock, I had the happiness of seeing that our voyage was nearly over; we were then coming upon the island of Sicily, and sailing flowly under the shelter of a great barren mountain. The entrance of the harbor is attended with some danger, as the wind, rushing suddenly on this side the mountain, which

which terminate abruptly, sometimes carries away the masts of the ships. The city of Palermo, from the sea, has a striking agreeable appearance. It is situated upon a small and fertile plain, backed by lofty mountains. Bright and cold. Wind N.W.

Palermo, *Feb.* 2.

This city, which is the capital of Sicily, is of great antiquity; and if a conjecture may be formed from its ancient name Panormus, which signifies an universal harbor, it was formerly in a very flourishing condition. By whom it was founded, is uncertain; nor have we any authentic accounts of its inhabitants till it became a colony of the Phenicians, after which it passed into the

the hands of the various nations that became masters of this island. The present city principally consists of two wide, uniform, and well built streets, each about a mile in length, crossing each other at right angles in the center, where there is a small octagon space, ornamented with four statues. Adjoining to the town, and near the sea, is a public garden or promenade, planted with orange and lemon-trees, formed into arcades, and now loaded with fruit; the stems of the trees stand in furrows, and are continually watered by a small stream. In the middle is a fountain, surrounded by four grotesque temples, in two of which are canary-birds. Among the oranges is a kind called sanguinei or bloody, which are stained in the middle with red, and have usually the finest flavor. Some of the lemons are sweet, but very flat, tasting like sugar and water. The citrons

citrons grow to an immenſe ſize; the rind, which occupies at leaſt three-fourths of the bulk of the fruit, is eaten with ſugar; the juice is ſharper than the foureſt lemon I ever taſted. Indian figs, in very great abundance, grow wild in the fields and hedges, to the height of twelve or fourteen feet; of theſe there are three kinds, one with large ſpines, another with ſmaller, and the third almoſt ſmooth. Their fruit is cooling and delicious, 10,000l. worth of which is ſold annually to the poor people in the neighbourhood of this city. Another plant, very common in this country, is the aloe, which uſually bloſſoms every fifth or ſixth year. Of theſe there are five or ſix ſpecies, which grow moſtly in the hedges, and, together with the Indian figs, form a moſt impenetrable fence.

In

In confequence of an introductory letter from Sir W. Hamilton, we have dined to day with the Prince Caramanico, viceroy of Sicily, who refided fome years in England as Ambaffador from the court of Naples. He has the command of all the troops in the ifland, and prefides over all the tribunals of juftice, and of the finances; in the quality of legate a latere from the Roman Pontiff, he fits under a canopy in the king's chapel, affifted by all the facred council. To him alfo belongs the nomination to all the municipal and military offices in the kingdom. He is an affable polite man, and notwithftanding the ftate in which he lives, made us feel ourfelves perfectly at eafe. He gave place to my brother, as a foreigner, but walked before all his other guefts. We fat down twenty to table, were ferved in great ftile ſtile and magnificence, and among a variety of other good things, had iced punch and Engliſh porter. The palace, which is an indifferent old building, is ſituated in a ſquare, near the ſouth gate of the city, and commands a delightful proſpect of the adjacent country. At the top is an obſervatory, inhabited by an ingenious old prieſt, who has been in England, and brought from thence ſeveral aſtronomical inſtruments conſtructed by Ramſden*. Bright and windy. Farenheit's thermometer, 63.

---

* In one of the rooms in the palace is a fire-place in which was a comfortable wood-fire, but I believe this is the only chimney in the whole iſland of Sicily, at leaſt, we never ſaw any other, either in the inſide or outſide of the beſt houſes and moſt magnificent palaces, except one in a convent of nobles, which, however, was never uſed. It is probable the viceroy borrowed the idea of his chimney and fire-place from what he had ſeen in England.

SINCE

Palermo, *Feb. 3.*

Since our arrival at this place, Captain Chianchi has done us the kindnefs to introduce us to Mr. Tough, an Englifh merchant, and banker, who refides here, and who takes infinite pains to oblige us in every way that lies in his power; with him we have been this evening at a Capuchin convent, about a mile out of town, in which is a vault made ufe of as a receptacle for the dead. It confifts of four wide paffages, each about forty feet in length, into which the light of the fun is admitted by windows at the ends. Along the fides of thefe are niches, in which the bodies are fet upright, cloathed in coarfe garments, with their heads, arms and feet bare. They are prepared for this fituation by broil-

broiling them six or seven months upon a gridiron, over a slow fire, till all the fat and moisture are consumed. The skin, which looks like pale coloured leather, remains entire, and the character of the countenance is in some degree preserved. A man who was with us, pointed out his father-in-law who had been dead two years; except the bodies of two reputed saints, one of which had been there 150 years, and the other 100, they are all of modern date, as appears by an inscription on a small piece of paste-board hung to the arms of every corpse, signifying the name of the person and the time of his decease. In some of the higher niches they are laid out at full length, and at the top are children of six or seven years of age. On the floor are handsome trunks, containing carcases of

per-

persons of distinction, the keys of which are kept by the relations. Cloudy and windy with storms of hail. Ther. 53.

PALERMO, *Feb.* 4.

THE magistrates appointed to preserve the order of society in this city, are, first, the supreme judge, to whom belongs the administration of justice in criminal cases; he is the head of the nobility, and immediately follows the viceroy in all the solemn functions. Secondly, the pretor, who regulates the affairs of the city. He is the perpetual deputy of the kingdom; chief in parliament of the order to whom appertains the right of regulating the king's demesne, and possessed of the prerogative of captain-general, during

during the absence of the viceroy. Thirdly, The pretorian court, which consists of three judges, citizens of Palermo, who are chosen annually by the king. They assist the supreme judge in the decision of criminal affairs, and the pretor in the deliberations upon the finances; these two officers, however, have neither vote nor signature, except the pretor, in the business respecting the public bank and first fruits. Fourthly, The senate of Palermo, composed of the pretor and six practitioners of the law, named by the king, who wear the toga after the manner of the ancient Roman senators, and principally inspect the police which regards the grain and provisions. There are, besides, seven great officers of state, to each of which is assigned a peculiar employment. First, *Il Maestro Portelano*, to whom is committed the care of of the public granaries, and who manages the sale of the corn both at home and abroad. The imposition of a tax upon this commodity has nearly proved the ruin of agriculture, especially as the exportation of it is prohibited to all those who are not able to pay an exorbitant price for that privilege. The quantity of corn annually produced in the island does not at present amount to more than a tenth part of what was collected in former years. Secondly, The auditor-general, who passes judgment, without appeal, upon all offences committed within the precincts of the palace. Thirdly, The high-admiral, whose jurisdiction extends over the marine. Fourthly, The chancellor, who overlooks all the notaries of the kingdom, prepares all official patents, reads the propositions when the parliament assembles, and, at the

the time of a coronation, tenders the oath of fidelity to the people, and alſo proclaims that of the monarch, who thereby binds himſelf to maintain and defend the privileges of the city of Palermo. The ſame ceremony takes place upon the inſtallation of a viceroy. Fifthly, The prothonotary of the queen's chamber, who has the inſpection of the demeſnes of ſix cities, viz. Syracuſe, Lentini, Carlentini, St. Filippo, Mineo and Virini, which were formerly appropriated to the queens of Sicily. Sixthly, The chief ſecretary, who preſides over the officers appointed to receive the taxes and duties in the places of their reſpective juriſdictions. And ſeventhly, The lieutenant of the royal exchequer, who has the adminiſtration of all effects that have been ſequeſtered or confiſcated.

This

This is the principal refidence of the greater part of the Sicilian nobility; and as it is not the cuftom for any gentleman to walk in the ftreets, at leaft 1000 carriages are faid to be kept in the town. They are for the moft part in the Englifh tafte, very elegant, and fhewn to the greateft advantage, with beautiful horfes richly caparifoned, and as many footmen in fplendid liveries as can be crowded together behind. Every evening all the people of rank drive about in this manner on the grand public terrace by the fea fide. There are alfo very convenient hackney coaches, covered and open, waiting all day in their refpective ftations.

The language fpoken here and throughout Sicily is Italian, nearly in the Neapolitan dialect, but in general better than at Naples. The cuftom alfo alſo of mixing much geſture in their diſcourſe, eſpecially with the head, fingers, or both, and more particularly when they are diſputing and quarrelling, is equally prevalent throughout Sicily as it is in Italy.

The number of taylors here is prodigious: the dreſs of the gentlemen is quite *a l'Angloiſe,* with frocks, round hats, and clubb'd hair, the modern faſhion of *cropping all round* having not yet reached Palermo.

The dreſs of the women of quality is nearly the ſame as in England and France; but their cuſtoms and manners quite of a piece with their Italian neighbours. The crime of adultery is ſo common, that no *Dama* of rank is thought the worſe of for being guilty of it.

The etiquette of the country is excellently well calculated to facilitate this kind of intercourse, it being reckoned highly ungenteel for any lady of diftinction to be feen in public with her own hufband, or without her admirer or cicifbeo, who alfo conftantly attends her when fhe goes out in her carriage, either by night or day.

Another thing which tends not a little to promote this fort of commerce, is the ftrefs laid by the priefts (in order to keep up the authority of the church) on breaches of human traditions, and mens inventions, fuch as non-attendance at mafs, neglecting an ave-maria, or eating flefh on a Friday or Saturday, rather than on thofe fins which are immediately againft the pofitive and revealed law of God. Thus by straining at gnats, little or no difficulty is made in swallowing camels.

And it is well if the great frequency of murders and assassinations, particularly at Naples and Rome*, may not in some measure be owing to the same cause, though the want of police and energy in the laws, and the commutation of punishment for money, as well as making the churches an asylum for murderers, may be the principal reasons for so many horrible butcherings in cool blood.

Both at Rome and Naples are hospitals for the stabbed, which are generally full. At Rome there are two, one for the men, another for the wo-

* During the last *holy week* at this place, full forty persons were sent reeking into eternity by the knife and stiletto.

men.

men. Few perfons go about without a ftiletto, and though the ufe of thefe deftructive weapons be prohibited by law, yet they are publicly expofed at the fhop windows, and may be bought by all forts of perfons without any queftions being afked.

While we were at Rome, the following curious converfation took place between my brother and his Lacquais de Place.

Sir R. H. Francefco, Have there been any perfons ftabbed to day?

Francefco. Certainly fome, but not fo many as in the holydays of the laft week, or as there will be on Sunday.

Sir R. H. Why fo?

Francefco. Becaufe to day is not a feftival, and the ufual time for ftabbing is, when quarrels arife among the people who are assembled to make merry, and drink together.

But as facts are beyond assertions, I shall here mention a few instances of what happened in our own knowledge during the time we were at Rome and Naples. A few days before our arrival at the latter place, a man's body was found in the street without an head, and I believe it was never known who was the murderer, or the person murdered. Indeed it is most likely no enquiry was ever made. The day after we came thither, Christmas day, two young women, sisters, were both stabbed in coming from mass about six o'clock in the morning. The one died on the spot, the other languished in great agonies for a day or two, and then expired. This deed was done by a sailor in a fit of jealousy.

Not

Not long after this, we faw a poor fellow weltering in his blood at the *Crocelle* door, a houfe where feveral Englifh families of diftinction lodged. He had been juft ftabbed by another who had a flight quarrel with him a day or two before, and who, as foon as he had wreaked his revenge, fled to a neighbouring church for refuge. A few days before we left Rome, an Englifh gentleman's coachman happening to have fome words with one of the under cooks of the hotel, whilft the carriage was waiting at the door; the fellow ran into the kitchen for his great knife, and inftantly flafhed him acrofs the belly, fo that his bowels came out; after which he wiped the bloody weapon with his apron, and went into the houfe. The coachman, who was an Italian, was carried to the hofpital, but expired the next day. We were told

told that he had been ſtabbed on different occaſions at leaſt thirty times before. The aſſaſſin, by the activity of the Engliſh gentlemen who lodged at the hotel, was apprehended and committed to priſon, but ſo long as he could raiſe any money, would probably eſcape the puniſhment due to his crime.

But to return to Palermo.—The ſurrounding mountains were this morning covered with ſnow, and ſome fell in the town: Thermometer at nine in the morning 40. The almond trees are covered with bloſſoms, but there is no other appearance of ſpring, though peaſe, beans, artichoaks, and immenſe cauliflowers, alſo excellent brocoli, with heads as large as the cauliflowers, come to perfection in the open fields all the winter.

PALERMO,

PALERMO, *Feb.* 5.

This day is commemorated throughout Sicily on account of the dreadful earthquake which destroyed Messina and the places adjacent just eight years ago, by which awful visitation of Providence upwards of 45,000 persons were destroyed. It was sensibly felt here, but did no damage on this side of the island.—The public places are shut up, and one day's humiliation substituted in the place of gaiety and dissipation.

We paid our respects this evening to the viceroy, who received us graciously, but like a sovereign prince, made the motion for us to withdraw; which we were told was his constant custom.

Mr. Tough, who has resided here these ten years, says this is the coldest season he has ever felt in this island.

The

The greateſt height of the thermometer, according to his obſervations, has been 118, and the loweſt 43; but yeſterday it was 55, and this morning at 36. It muſt have been ſtill lower without the city, as the ſmall pools were covered with ice.

PALERMO, *Feb. 6.*

IT was our intention to have left this place yeſterday morning, but we are detained by bad weather, very much againſt our inclinations, in a moſt filthy inn, which has, however, the reputation of being the beſt in the town. We are confined in a ſmall room, without a fire-place, and with one window, much out of repair, almoſt covered with dirt and cobwebs. The greater

greater part is occupied by two wretched beds, and the remaining fpace by three chairs and a table, upon which we eat our meals, which, though by no means calculated to pleafe the epicure or the glutton, are fufficient to fatisfy the cravings of hunger. For this apartment, and another not quite fo good, we pay full three guineas and an half a week, and near five fhillings a-piece for our miferable repaft at dinner, fervants apart. It was the landlady of this inn that Mr. Brydone has fo humouroufly defcribed in his thirty-firft letter: She has been dead fome years, but her hufband is ftill alive, and properly calculated to be the turnkey of his own prifon. As we purpofed returning to Palermo after our intended expedition, we have requefted him to take the charge of our cloaths during our abfence, which he abfolutely refufes

to

to do, unlefs we will pay the fame price for their lodging as for our own; a demand with which we do not choofe to comply. Cold, with ftorms of hail and wind.

FAVOROTTA, *Feb.* 7.

BEFORE I begin any defcription of our journey into the other parts of this ifland, it may be proper to premife a few circumftances refpecting its general hiftory.

The firft inhabitants of this country, were the Leftrygones and the Cyclopes, the accounts of which are fo mingled with fable, that we have nothing authentic upon record concerning them; the next were the Sicani,

from

from whence the island was called Sicanus, instead of its former name, Trinacria, which was given to it on account of its triangular shape. These people were afterwards confined to the western part of the island. Some Trojans, after the burning of their city, came and settled near them, and built Erix and Egesta; these assumed the name of Elymæi, and were afterwards joined by some inhabitants of Phocis, at their return from the siege of Troy. The Siculi came in great numbers from Italy; and, having gained a considerable victory over the Sicani, confined them to a corner of their island, about three hundred years before the arrival of the Greeks. From them the island was called Sicily. The Phœnicians also spread themselves along the coast, and in the little islands, which border upon it for the convenience of trade; but

after

after the Greeks began to fettle there, they retired into the country of the Elymæi, to be near Carthage, and abandoned the reft. The firft of the Greeks that croffed over into Sicily, were the Chalcedians of Eubœa, under Theocles, who founded Naxos. This was in the year of the world 3293, and 711 before the birth of Chrift. After the Greeks came the Carthaginians, and after them the Romans, who reduced all Sicily to a Roman province. It was afterwards ravaged by the Saracens and the Goths, the latter of whom brought the whole ifland into their fubjection; but it was recovered by the Romans, under Narfes, Anno Chrifti, 553. As the Roman empire declined, the Saracens recommenced their ravages; but the pope, with the affiftance of other Chriftian powers, again drove them out; in which fervice,

Tan-

Tancred the Norman and his twelve fons, having had a great fhare, part of Naples was given them by the pope. Robert, the fon of Tancred, was created duke of Apulia and Calabria, by the German emperor; and Roger, the fon of Robert, was made king of the two Sicilies, viz. Naples and Sicily. The heirs of Tancred enjoyed this crown until the year 1166, when, happening to difoblige the pope, he introduced the earl of Anjou and the French, and his pofterity were kings of Naples and Sicily, until the Spaniards difpoffeffed them of it, about the year 1504. The Spaniards held the dominion till 1707, when they were driven from thence by the Imperialifts; and at the peace of Utrecht, this ifland was allotted to the duke of Savoy, with the title of king. The Spaniards invaded it in 1718, but were forced to abandon it again, and

then

then it was conferred on the emperor Charles the VIth, who held it till the year 1735, when the Imperialifts were driven out of this ifland, and of all their Italian dominions, and Don Carlos, the king of Spain's eldeft fon, by the princefs of Parma, his fecond queen, was advanced to the throne of the two Sicilies, which were confirmed to him by a fubfequent peace, on condition of his relinquifhing Milan, Parma, and all the reft of the emperor's Italian dominions, which the Spaniards and French had taken from him in that war, and Don Carlos, fucceeding his brother Ferdinand the VIth, as king of Spain, Ferdinand his third fon, is now king of the two Sicilies.

After having had a moft alarming defcription of the roads, inns, and manner of travelling in this country, and

and after having been informed of desperate gangs of robbers, that infect every part of the island, we set out from Palermo at half past eight this morning, to prove the truth or falsehood of the relations that had been given us. The equipage provided for my brother and myself, is called a litiga, which is a sort of sedan coach, or *vis-a-vis*, supported by two poles, and carried by mules. This litiga, or double sedan, has no glass in the windows, but thick curtains in case of rain, neither has it any doors, but you are lifted in and out through the windows, by the men holding a little board for you to put your foot on. The sides are painted with superstitious devices, to secure you from dangers: among these, the virgin and child, and the souls in purgatory, are seldom omitted.

The like is on all their boats, particularly on what are called, the *fproronara*.

My nephew and our servants are furnished with good horses; three or four other men accompany us to take care of the beasts, and we have, besides, a soldier for our guard, with a gun and cutlass, so that we conceive ourselves able to make a pretty strong resistance in case of an attack. For the first seven miles, we travelled upon an excellent carriage road, over the plain, which is ornamented with country houses and gardens, corn fields, now beautifully green, groves of exceeding fine olives, and stately orange and lemon trees, loaded with fine fruit, and some other garden trees, most of which are in blossom, particularly almonds, plumbs, and peaches. We next passed over a very rugged road, under rocks

rocks by the sea-side, and by hedges of large aloes, many of which had flowered last year. The stems of several more were cut down, and used for gate-posts and other purposes. This plant, as also the Indian fig, are both extremely hardy, and will florish on the tops of walls, on the sides of rocks and mountains, and even in the most barren sand. The manner of making hedges, is by sticking a single leaf of the Indian fig into the ground, which soon takes root, and grows to a great size; when old, it has a bark formed round it, consisting of its first leaves, grown hard and become brown. This is perhaps the only tree or shrub known that is raised by the leaves, which grow one out of another for some years before it has any stem or scarcely any root.

Our whole day's journey has been twenty-two miles, and we are now at a small town confisting of fix or feven wide parallel ftreets, the houfes of which are all poor, and only one ftory high. Such is our inn, which, to our aftonifhment, is perfectly clean, and contains three beds, upon which we may venture to fleep, without apprehenfions. Befides a moft admirable arrangement of crockery ware, the walls are ornamented with images, crucifixes, and pictures of faints; and, as a farther proof of the piety of the two good old women that keep the houfe, there is a figure of a little waxen virgin juft delivered, with the infant Jefus lying by her, carefully preferved in a glafs cafe; though this figure of the virgin lies proftrate, kicking up the legs in no very decent manner, yet we fhould certainly have been thought highly

pro-

profane, had we made any animadverfions on it. The windows are not glazed, and we have no other defence againſt the cold, which is at preſent pretty ſevere, but wooden ſhutters, which, for the advantage of the light, we keep open. There is no food of any kind in the houſe, excepting ſome that we brought with us from Palermo, and which we are now going to dreſs ourſelves, over a charcoal brazier in the middle of the room. Froſty morning. Bright cool day.

CASTELL A MARE, *Feb.* 8.

WE ſet out this morning in the ſame ſtyle as yeſterday, and continuing our route to the weſtward, coaſted a very fine bay, twenty-two miles to this place.

place. The country is well cultivated, producing large groves of olives, some plantations of the manna tree, from whence the manna is extracted by making incisions in the bark; it issues from the wound as a thick whitish liquor, which soon hardens in the sun, when it is carefully taken off and gathered into boxes. The usual time of procuring it is the month of August, when the heat is most violent. There is besides a great deal of corn, and a few vineyards. Some land is left for pasturage, in which are fed great numbers of sheep, goats, and horned cattle. The sheep and goats are black and white, or white entirely, with long silky hair. The horned cattle, particularly the oxen, are small, of the same reddish brown as those in England, and have remarkably large horns,

stand-

ſtanding more upright than the horns of theſe animals uſually do.

This is a poor little town, ſituated at the foot of an high, rocky mountain, the upper part of which is barren, but the lower is cultivated with corn, and forms a beautiful lawn, on which are ſome fine ſpreading evergreens.

Travellers muſt expect great difficulties. We now experience the miſeries of viſiting a country where roads and inns are hardly known. We are got into an houſe it is true, but it is filthy in the extreme, and we are again expoſed to the ſeverities of a cold air iſſuing through unglazed windows, and creeks and crevices in every quarter of the ſhattered edifice. Even here, however, we are not without luxuries, as we are going to ſup upon a turtle

which

which we purchased this morning for twenty pence. There are many of these animals in the Sicilian seas, but as the English method of cooking calipash and calipee is unknown, their flesh is not much esteemed. Cool and cloudy.

HOVEL, 10*th*.

WE laid ourselves down last night upon mattrasses of straw as hard as boards, and endeavoured to take some repose after the fatigues of the day; but our first efforts to sleep were interrupted by people walking backwards and forwards through the room, and our second, by legions of fleas, who, as soon as we grew warm, crawled about us in every direction, and kept us us in a state of continual restlessness till the happy hour of rising. The woman of this house disposed of a young child in a way that must be very convenient to poor people with large families; viz. by laying it in a cloth, and suspending it by four cords to the *cieling*, I should say the *roof*, which was composed of canes laid across the beams.

We found ourselves the spectacle of the place, and were surrounded at night by some well-drest people, who ought to have had more politeness, and in the morning by the fishermen of the town, in whose baskets were some small fish, variegated with the most beautiful colours; one among them, called *Il pesce del re*, or, the king's fish, was of a bright green and gold, with a zig-zag stripe of red down each side.

We

We set out again this morning for Segesta, distant nine miles, and travelled on a very bad, stony road, over mountains on which are some groves of olives, manna trees, and common figs, and from whence we had a view of an extensive vale cultivated with corn, but thinly inhabited.

The city of Segesta was founded by the Trojans, as has been already observed. It was by them called Egesta, but the Romans, disliking so unpropitious a name, (Egesta signifying want or poverty) afterwards changed it to that which it now bears. A dispute between the people of this city and their neighbours, the Selinuntians, occasioned one of the most memorable wars that was ever waged in Sicily. The territories of the two cities were divided by a river, which the Selinuntians

tians croffed, and poffeffed themfelves of the lands lying next to it. Upon this the Egeftans took up arms, and repulfed the invaders, who fhortly afterwards returned with an army and laid wafte the whole country. The Egeftans again armed themfelves in their own defence, but were entirely defeated, and forced to fhelter themfelves within their walls. In this condition they fent ambaffadors to folicit fuccours from Agrigentum, Syracufe, and even Carthage; but thefe embaffies proving unfuccefsful, they implored the affiftance of the Athenians, promifing, that they, in their turn, would help them to the utmoft of their power, whenever they fhould ftand in need of their affiftance. They reprefented, among other things, that fhould they be abandoned, the Syracufans, by whom the inhabitants of Selinus were affifted,

affifted, would feize their city as they had done that of Leontium, and make themfelves mafters of the whole ifland. The Athenians, who had long waited for an opportunity of interfering in the affairs of Sicily, agreed to the propofals. However, they thought it advifeable firft to fend deputies into Sicily, to inquire into the ftate of the ifland, and particularly of the Egeftans, who had promifed to pay all the troops that fhould be fent to their affiftance. Upon the arrival of the ambaffadors, the Egeftans, having borrowed from the neighbouring nations a great number of gold and filver vafes, made a vain fhew of them, faying, they had wealth fufficient to defray the whole charges of the war. The Athenians, deceived by thefe appearances, fent a fleet to Sicily, under the command of Alcibiades, Nifias, and Lamachus. Upon on their arrival at Rhegium, they sent some ships to cruize off the coast of Sicily, in order to find out a proper and convenient place for landing the troops, and at the same time to know what treasure the Egestans could contribute towards carrying on the war which had been undertaken for their sake. These, on their return, acquainted the generals, that the Egestans had imposed upon them, and abused their credulity, since they were a poor indigent people, and had only thirty talents in the public treasury. However disconcerted the Athenian generals were at this intelligence, they resolved not to return ingloriously to their own country, but sailed for Sicily, and took Catania by surprize; they soon after advanced towards Syracuse, against which they carried on a long and bloody war, with various success, cefs, till at laft victory declared in favor of the Syracufans, fome particulars of which I fhall mention in my account of that celebrated city.

All that now remains of Segefta, is one Doric temple, confifting of thirty-fix pillars; two rows of fourteen each from the length, and two of fix the breadth. Each pillar is compofed of feveral ftones, laid like mill-ftones upon one another. They are all in their original ftate of perfection, except three or four, which were repaired in 1781 at the king's expence, as appears by an infcription of white marble placed in front of the building, though in the opinion of moft this modern reparation had better have been let alone, as well as what has been done in the fame way at Pompeia, near Naples.

But

But his Sicilian majefty has certainly a much better tafte for maccaroni, which he devours in vaft quantities, even with the *lazaroni*, or common people, than he has for antiquities or improvements.

Next to eating maccaroni, the favourite amufements of the Neapolitan monarch are hunting and fhooting; though the blifs he obtains from the latter, muft be of a very uncommon kind, as will be evident from the manner in which his majefty purfues, or rather murders his game.

If the object of the royal vengeance be pheafants, he has three or four hundred of thefe poor animals, which are as tame as barn-door fowls, (particularly at his hunting feat in the little ifland of Procita) confined within a
fmall

small inclosed compass, himself being seated in an alcove above, by the front of which the *chasseurs* drive the birds one after another, without a minute's delay, whilst his majesty fires at them as fast as he can discharge his pieces, and when he is tired of the excellent sport, boasts that he has killed with his own hand two or three hundred pheasants in an hour's time. This intelligence we got from the King's own *garde de chasse* on the spot at Procita.

That the late king had precisely the same *penchant* for the sports of the field with his present majesty, and that he at least paid as much attention to the preservation of his game, the following anecdote will fully evince.

Not many years ago he ordered all the cats in the island of Procita to be destroyed,

destroyed, under the idea that they killed his pheasants; this bloody sentence was executed with rigor, but the inhabitants soon became sensible of its bad effects, for the rats and mice multiplied to such a degree, that the whole produce of the island was in danger, and the former even attacked the children in their cradles. A petition was presented to the king, setting forth the grievance, to which his majesty immediately gave ear, and made another decree in favour of the cats, who soon did their duty so well, that though the pheasants do not appear at all diminished, there are few rats to be seen.

This island of Procita was once part of a Grecian colony, and to this day all the women and girls wear the ancient Grecian dress, which is very singular and becoming. At our request two or three

three females adorned themselves in their holyday cloaths. We had beds in the palace, but alas! alas! we had quite too many bedfellows of the hopping and creeping kind, *pidocchi, cimici, & pulci da vero.* When *la caccia de cinghiale,* or hunting and shooting the wild boar is the diversion his Majesty fixes on, and which he usually prefers to all others, he then sometimes goes to Astroni, near Naples, where in the crater of an extinct volcano, three miles in circumference, but which is now filled with noble timber trees, are several hundreds of those animals, which flock in droves to be fed at the keeper's whistle, though we were obliged to conceal ourselves behind a wall to prevent their seeing us. This wall, however, which was so friendly to our curiosity, is very inimical to the poor boars, as the king stations himself

self behind it in order to shoot them, and will sometimes massacre fifty or an hundred in a day. He then registers his feats in a book, mentioning both the number and the size of the boars he has killed with his own hand. As a proof of this king's extraordinary piety, a newspaper would say *Piety extraordinary*, when madness was in his kennels, he made the poor quadrupeds hear mass, put his hand into their mouths, and said he was certain no hurt could then befal him or them. This we had from one who is honoured with his particular friendship and attention.

What exquisite taste his majesty has for the fine arts, evidently appears by the paintings in his grand palace at Caserta, the apartments of which are adorned with pictures of his different sea-ports, and representations of his hunting

hunting the wild boars, in moſt of which the king himſelf makes the principal figure. The royal orders are, that the colors muſt be all bright and glaring, without any ſhade or ſoftening whatever. But as this mandate cauſes ſome of the ſtate rooms to look as if they were hung with ſhew-boards for a puppet-ſhew, ſo it ſadly fetters the genius of that very able artiſt Mr. Hackert, who has the honor of being the king's firſt painter.

While I am relating theſe anecdotes of the king of Naples, I muſt not forget to add that he is very popular in his own capital, is quite adored and idolized by the *lazaroni,* or common people, who, whenever he has been abſent, go out by thouſands to draw his carriage, and to ſhout his welcome return, and that both he and his queen are

are exceedingly polite and condefcending to ftrangers.

My long digreffion has brought me fo far back to Naples and its environs, that I had almoft forgotten I was vifiting the famous Doric temple of Segefta; I therefore haften back to that temple, the dimenfions of which I had not an opportunity of examining with any degree of accuracy, as an heavy rain commenced juft upon our arrival, and obliged us to take fhelter for more than two hours in a miferable hovel. As it was at the fame time very cold, we lighted a fire on the floor, the fmoke of which almoft fuffocated us; however, to make us amends, the fhepherd of the hut regaled us with curds and whey made of goats and fheeps milk. Not being very well contented with our quarters, we set out again in the rain, which, however, ceased before we arrived at the bottom of the mountain, so that we flattered ourselves with the hopes of getting a better lodging than could be obtained at Castell à Mare. But we soon found a very unexpected difficulty. A brook, which three hours before was but a very insignificant stream, was now become impassable. We would gladly have gone to Alcamo, a town only a few miles distant, where we knew there was a good inn, but our guides soon cut that scheme short, by telling us it lay on the other side of the water. Under their direction we went to another hut about half a mile off, which was the dwelling of an honest farmer, who was gone out, and had fastened the door, which they broke open without the least ceremony. This habitation is rather better than that

upon

upon the top of the hill, and contains two apartments, one of which we nearly enjoy to ourselves, having no other company than our guard and his favorite horse. In an hour's time the rain began again, and has continued all night, with an high wind. A large heap of reeds laid in one corner of the place has afforded us something like a bed, in which we have not indeed been infested with the same kind of vermin as at Castell à Mare, but with rats, immense wasps, and spiders in abundance *. As a defence against the cold,

---

* Though there are large spiders in Sicily of an horrible appearance, having legs all round their bodies, yet I believe there are none of that particular quality which are found near Tarentum, and from thence called tarantula, the bite of which is supposed to be cured by music and dancing. As in our passage through Calabria we were at no great distance from Tarentum, we made some inquiries about this species of spider, the poison of which is almost generally believed in those parts to be extracted

cold, a fire upon the floor was kept burning all night, and our benevolent guard, wishing us to keep ourselves warm within as well as without, pressed us repeatedly to drink wine, which he drew from the farmer's casks

or charmed away by this remedy, which is often tried by the country people, when they really are, or when they fancy themselves bitten by these animals, and I have no doubt usually proves succesful through the force of imagination, and the violent exercise and profuse sweats attending these dancings, which are continued for several hours without interruption, and this usually in the midst of summer, as the tarantula is said to bite worse in the harvest months, when the common people are working in the fields, and not aware of the attack.

As I am now mentioning Tarentum, it may not be out of the way to observe that the breed of fine snow-white sheep, so celebrated by the ancient poets for their excellence, and for being washed in the river Galesus, now no longer exists. On the contrary they are almost all black; what may have been the cause of this great change from one color to its direct opposite, is not perhaps very easy to determine. The notion there prevalent, that it is owing to all the white sheep being poisoned by eating a certain herb which grows in the neighborhood, and which yet does no injury to the black sheep, is not a very probable one.

as

as often as he thought proper. It is now seven in the morning, and I perceive very little prospect of passing the brook to day. Thank God we none of us yet suffer from cold or fatigue, but dread the thought of passing another night in this miserable situation.

PALERMO, *Feb.* 12.

ABOUT half past seven yesterday morning a messenger was sent to see if the waters were abated, who brought word back that the river was full six feet deep; it was consequently impossible for our carriage, not raised more than three feet from the ground, to pass. It still rained, though the violence of the storm was abated; and I began to be seriously afraid of a second or more engagements with the Sicilian rats, wafps and fpiders, which no doubt fo much company, and the large fire we had kept burning all night on the floor, had roufed from their different quarters. As all our ftock of bread and meat was exhaufted, and as nothing remained but a few little fifh, which we brought with us from Caftell à Mare, we difpatched a meffenger in queft of food. He returned about eleven with fome bread and a live kid, the latter of which we fuppofe he ftole; we could not confent to the death of the poor animal, nor had we any occafion for it, as we were then diverted from our cookery by the agreeable intelligence that the brook was paffable; we therefore fet out as foon as poffible, and got acrofs without any difficulty. In returning over the mountains we met with fuch violent ftorms storms of hail and rain, that our muleteers were very defirous of returning to Caftell à Mare, but we, willing to get back to Palermo without further hindrance, infifted upon going on. They complied with reluctance, alledging there would be no boat at a ferry about a mile diftant. They faid true; however, by fair words and large promifes, we prevailed upon the ferryman to prepare his veffel, and began to flatter ourfelves that all the difficulties of the journey were over, when he greatly damped our fpirits by affirming, in a very pofitive manner, that we fhould not be able to proceed much farther without finding other rivers, which he was fure would impede our paffage. While we were holding a confultation upon the beft mode of proceeding, we fpied a man and horfe on the other fide. The man told us he

he had paffed the rivers, and as the rain then ceafed, we ventured to purfue our journey, and arrived in fafety at a fmall village eight miles from Caftell à Mare, where the conductors of ourfelves and cattle determined we fhould pafs the night. We found one little room, tolerably clean, at leaft not exceedingly filthy, and well covered, but with an open window, like all the reft in Sicily. It contained one bed, which, though pretty large, could not conveniently accommodate us all at a time, fo that we were obliged to repofe ourfelves by turns; unfortunately for us the man of the houfe was very deaf, and his wife, who did the honors, bawled fo loud, that we were almoft ftunned. We met here with fome very rich lufcious wine, which our guards drank off as if it were fmall-beer, though ficknefs and head-
ach

ach were the effects of their indulgence.

As soon as day appeared, we set out again, dined with the clean women at Favorotta, and came hither this evening, hoping to go soon and comfortably to bed, having been four nights without undressing. Our banker had promised to use his endeavours to procure us a lodging, but had none in readiness; our old apartments were occupied, and we were told at two other inns that there was no room for us. After much solicitation and inquiry, we have at length obtained one apartment at what in Sicily may be called a good inn, and which is at least much better than our last, kept by a noisy Frenchwoman, who seems very sorry that it is not in her power to accommodate us better. An hour and half ago we ordered supper

per to be got ready with all poſſible expedition, but do not yet ſee the leaſt preparation for it. Cold and windy.

―――――――

PALERMO, *Feb.* 13.

AFTER waiting four hours for ſupper laſt night, and then underſtanding that the old cock was not boil'd half tender, and that its companion on the ſpit was not put down to roaſt, we went to bed not very well pleaſed with our new inn. The landlady is between fifty and ſixty years of age, very plain, and immenſely fat, and as ſhe dreſſes in a garment once white, but now abominably dirty, without ſtays, and her clotted hair hangs over her eyes like the ſnakes of a Meduſa's head, ſhe is not one of the moſt engaging

gaging figures in the world. She is very vociferous, full of action, and extremely indelicate. Laſt night we miſſed a bottle of Syracuſe wine, which ſhe owned having drank; it had the effect that might be expected, and one of our ſervants, who had the audacity to contradict her, received ſo ſevere a ſcolding from the enraged lady, that he thought it moſt prudent to allow ſhe was perfectly in the right. She was very ſick all night, and this morning made an apology for her behavior, acknowledging, " She was really ſo " drunk that ſhe did not know what " ſhe did." This ſweet creature is not without a partner; he is a good looking young man, about twenty-three, and was, at the time of *her* propoſal, (for it originated entirely from the lady) a lay-brother in a convent. " To " own the truth (ſaid ſhe) I fell in
" love

"love with him, and I married him." In our apartment there is a picture of this lovely lady, whofe charms are fet off to the beft advantage. Her head is dreffed high, with a feather and a blue bandeau; at one corner of the mouth, which expreffes an *agreeable* fmile, is a little black patch. The breaft is bare, and the waift drawn into as fmall a compafs as is confiftent with the other parts, though the painter has very judicioufly expreffed the effects of tight lacing by the exaltation of certain protuberances above the ftays. In her right hand, which is held up with an elegant turn of the little finger, fhe holds a full blown rofe, intended, no doubt, as the juft emblem of her own charms.

The number of inhabitants in this city, is computed at 320,000, which is is so immense, compared with the size of the place, that I could not have credited it, unless I had heard it from the mouth of several well informed persons, and there is little doubt, but that this number would still encrease, if there were roads to communicate with the other parts of the island, and if the weight of taxes, under which the people groan, did not occasion the almost total abolition of trade.

The accounts we have had of the banditti, are not void of foundation, though they are by far, less numerous than formerly, many having been dispersed and executed within a few years. Such of them as surrender themselves voluntarily, are pardoned, upon condition of enlisting in the king's service. There are many who have embraced the proposal, and these are the *campieri,* or guards, that attend upon travellers. They are acquainted with all the banditti of the island, and are always faithful to those they take the charge of, for though they will rob, and even murder others, their employers may rest perfectly secure, under their protection, as they pique themselves on being MEN OF STRICT HONOR. Our guard, who is a fine stout young man, is one of the foregoing description, and though he made free with the farmer's wine, the poor kid, and some few things besides, at the places where we stopt, we found him to us, honest, civil, and good humoured, as well as exceedingly useful, in every respect. There is a convent of noble monks, seven miles from this city, who keep sixteen of these fellows, in constant pay, and are attended by one or more of them in all their excursions.

fions. When a robber is taken, he is brought into town mounted upon a mule, and guarded by thefe foldiers, who fire guns as they pafs through the ftreets, while the criminal, having his head crowned with flowers, is made a fpectacle to the people. Common criminals fuffer death, by hanging, and are executed naked. People of rank are beheaded. The power of the ax does not depend upon the ftrength of the executioner, but the fteel or iron part is fixed on a frame, and, being made to fall with great force, fevers the head from the body in a moment. The laft perfon that fuffered in that way, was a page of the viceroy, who committed murder in the palace. He had an intrigue with another man's wife, and, finding the hufband too much in the way, invited him one evening to drink a difh of coffee with him. As foon as he he came in, the page locked the door, murdered his gueſt by ſtabbing him in ſixteen places, and then went out, leaving the corpſe locked up in his room. The murderer continued about the town, but being miſſed in his place, at the palace, enquiry was made after him, and his room door forced open, four days after the commiſſion of the fact, when the corpſe was found in a ſtate of putrefaction. He was ſoon after taken, and met with the puniſhment which his crime deſerved. I am ſorry to remark, that he is not the only perſon of ſome note in this city, chargeable with the crime of murder. Laſt year, many people in this town and neighborhood, died in a ſudden and extraordinary manner; they were generally ſeized with vomiting, and expired in a few hours. The cauſe of their death was diſcovered in the following manner. A young woman

man went to an officer of juftice, to make fome complaints concerning her hufband; he defired her to be reconciled, and refufed to proceed againft him, upon which, fhe turned away in a rage, muttering, that fhe knew how to be revenged. The magiftrate paid attention to what fhe faid, and gave orders for her being arrefted; when, upon ftrict enquiry concerning the meaning of her words, fhe confeffed, that it was her intention to poifon her hufband, by purchafing a bottle of vinegar from an old woman, who prepared it for that purpofe. In order to afcertain the truth of this ftory, another woman was fent to the old jade, to demand fome of the fame vinegar, which was fold for about ten-pence a bottle. " What do you want with it?" faid the vender, " Why," (replied the other) " I have a very bad hufband, and I "want to get rid of him." Hereupon, the old woman, seventy-two years of age, produced the fatal dose, upon which she was immediately seized, and conducted to prison, where she confessed, that she had sold forty-five or forty-six bottles. Many people were taken up, but as upon further enquiry it was discovered that several of the nobility had been purchasers, the affair was dropt, and the old woman alone suffered death. Fair and cool.

Feb. 14.

THE plain on which Palermo stands, extends eight or nine miles, both to the east and west, behind two great rocky mountains, which are placed like bas-tions upon the two extremities of an hand-

handsome bay. We have been this morning on the eastern side, called La Bagaria, where several of the nobility have their country seats *. The palace of Palagonia is one of the most curious, and was formerly much more so, when in the possession of a *principe* of that name, who died a few years ago. Some specimens of his taste however, still remain, particularly a large collection of statues, fixed upon the walls of some low buildings, that form a semicircular court behind his house; these have, at least, an air of novelty, to recommend them to the curious traveller, who in all the fine collections of antiques, preserved at

* It may almost be said, without deviating from the strictest truth, that the houses in this neighbourhood are formed of shells, as the quarries from whence the materials for building are collected, contain an immense quantity of minute fossils consolidated together, with very few stony particles in proportion to the general mass.

Rome, and other cities in Italy, can difcover none like thofe, that difplay the extraordinary genius of this illuftrious and whimfical Sicilian. They are hewn by the hand of a modern mafon, into the fhape of men and women, fome playing on fiddles, flutes, bafs-viols, and fome with big bellies, wooden legs, enormous heads, and diftorted countenances. Other figures are ftill more fingular. An afs's head (fome may fay, no uncommon thing) upon a man's fhoulders, a bird's neck upon a lady's waift, with almoft every other fpecies of monfter, that it is poffible to conceive. Thefe are crowded together, as clofe as they can ftand, and feem much better calculated to fupport the building upon which they are erected, than the building them. The infide of the palace is commodious, but not magnificent, and has been

almoft

almoſt as whimſical as the outſide. The remains of the ancient taſte, appear in an apartment fitted up in the Chineſe ſtyle, with china pots, little images, pieces of different coloured glaſs and gilded ornaments, which altogether have not a bad effect. The cieling is coved, and covered over with looking-glaſſes. In another apartment are marble figures of the prince, princeſs, and others of the family, placed in compartments of the wall, in long flowing wigs and laced ruffles. About a quarter of a mile diſtant, is the palace of another noble Sicilian, fitted up in an elegant ſtyle, and is upon the whole, a very comfortable habitation. In the compartments of one of the rooms, the prints given in Captain Cook's Voyages, are copied in colors, and in an adjoining apartment, is the buſt of that navigator, as alſo one of Newton. Before the

the houfe is a fine terrace commanding a delightful profpect, both of fea and land, and about one hundred yards higher, a very fingular rock, not unlike thofe painted in India papers, ornamented with fruit trees, and Indian figs. On the top is a heavy temple, to which there is a road, broad enough for two carriages to pafs, fenced by a maffy wall. The gardens are all in the French ftyle, only, if poffible, more formal. Bright and cool.

PALERMO, *Feb.* 15.

HAVING obtained a recommendation from the viceroy, to the monks of St. Martino, we were conducted this morning, by one of the brethren and Mr. Tough to the convent. It is feven miles

miles from the town, in a very elevated ſituation facing the north, and backed by a mountain, now covered with ſnow. None but noblemen's ſons are made members of the fraternity; they are ſent thither young for education, and at the expiration of ſeven years, are obliged either to turn monks, or knights of Malta, who, as well as thoſe that lead a monaſtic life, make a vow of chaſtity. The magnificence of the convent is much ſuperior to any thing of the kind I have yet ſeen; it has lately been rebuilt, and 159,000 crowns expended upon it, to which many more muſt be added for the completion of the plan. The entrance is through an hall, ſupported by marble pillars, from whence on the right hand, goes a very ſpacious and magnificent double ſtair-caſe, of Sicilian marble, leading to the apartments of the ſuperior, the walls of
which

which are most elegantly painted in fresco. The galleries leading to the different chambers appear as long as the sides of the Bodleian library at Oxford. At the end of one of them, a fountain half enclosed with laurels has a pleasing effect. The library is an handsome room, supported by Corinthian pillars, made of walnut-tree, finely polished. Among the books, I observed the works of Hufs, Beza, Melancthon, and Calvin, and on the next shelf, those of Crellius and Socinus. In a small room, denominated the museum, are several curiosities, viz. armour of the Saracens, Sicilian coins, Gothic pictures, Grecian earthenware, particularly a large dish, with battles drawn in different compartments, fossils, a stuffed crocodile, about six feet long, taken in the island, monsters, manuscripts, &c. Among the manuscripts is one in the

Mo-

Morocco language containing an account, that the Saracens, upon coming into this iſland, firſt took poſſeſſion of the convent of Saint Martino, and killed thirty of the monks. There are only ten belonging to the fraternity at preſent, and thoſe are divided into two parties, hating each other moſt cordially; and rich as they are, being ready to devour one another on account of pelf and power. Owing to theſe animoſities all the workmen have been diſmiſſed from the convent.

After having ſeen every thing worthy of notice, we ſat down to a very elegant dinner*, conſiſting of two courſes

---

* Firſt courſe. A tureen at top and bottom, containing, in one, gravy ſoup, in the other, macaroni and cheeſe. On one ſide boulli, on the oppoſite woodcock pye. At the four corners were paties, and different made diſhes, chiefly in paſtry. Second courſe. Red mullets,

courses and a desert, with a frame of ornamental china, adorned with flowers, down the middle of the table, and were plentifully served with wine by the chief butler, who always held the bottle in his hand, and replenished our glasses whenever we did but sip at their contents. Four monks, one stranger, and ourselves sat down to dinner, but only two of the monks eat any thing; the two others (Mr. Tough told us) had dined before, and would not eat with us because we were not recommended to their party. When they have no company, the rules of the convent oblige them to dine together,

mullets, roast fowls, rasoles, a pudding made of pistachio nuts, which grow in great plenty in this island, &c. &c. &c. A desert followed of seventeen things, among which were two plates with thin slices of raw bacon, one of anchovies, one of cheese, one of fennel, and one of celery; afterwards came ices, and then coffee. So much for the mortification and self-denial of our noble religionists.

and the rules of envy, hatred and malice which thefe holy brothers have eftablifhed, oblige them to keep their feparate places, and never to converfe together. The monk that conducted us we difcovered to be a brother mafon, but we were defired not to mention it at the convent, as the oppofite party were not of that fraternity. We obferved one waiting at table in a monk's habit, and, till we heard his hiftory, felt fhocked at being ferv'd by a perfon of fo much dignity. He had been a merchant, was married, and had feveral children; a diffolute life caufed him to fail in bufinefs: His creditors were importunate, and the neceffities of his family very preffing; to avoid both he took fhelter in this convent, was admitted as a lay-brother, and lives here unmolefted by the creditors duns, and infenfible to the cries of his afflicted

afflicted family. It is not to be supposed that prayers and masses form the sole employment in this religious house; some recreations are allowed, such as billiards, shooting, and the like. The studious (though I believe there is only *one* of that description at present) amuse themselves in the library: The rest are completely ignorant, and notwithstanding their profession, disbelieve every article of revelation. About a month ago an opera girl, dress'd in man's cloaths, got admission into the convent, and came in with four men. The porter observing only four go out, asked where their companion was; they said he was coming, but as there was no appearance of him for some time, the porter began to entertain suspicions; he therefore gave an alarm, and after some search, the lady was found in a room below stairs, belonging to to one of the servants. The man said he did not know who it was that came in, and all the monks of course denied having any knowledge of the affair. Bright and cold, which we felt very severely, being obliged to sit upon Dutch tiles, without a fire, and with the windows and doors wide open. Therm. at sun rise, 43.

PALERMO, *Feb.* 16.

I TOOK a very laborious walk this morning to the top of Monte Pelegrino, the bastion on the west. Near the summit were found the bones of Saint Rosalia, the tutelary saint of Palermo, who is honored every year with one of the most splendid festivals in all the Roman Catholic countries. She was (as tradition and Mr. Brydone inform us)

daughter

daughter of William the Good, and retired to this mountain in the fifteenth year of her age, to spend the remainder of her life in solitude and devotion. She soon after disappeared, and it was supposed that she had been translated to heaven, till in the year 1624, four hundred and sixty-five years afterwards, during the time of a plague, it was revealed to an holy man, in a vision, that the saint's bones were lying in a cave, and that if they were taken up, and carried in procession thrice round the walls of the city, they should be delivered from the plague. At first little attention was paid to this account, but as the holy man persisted in his story, search was made, the bones found, and the city delivered from its calamity. For the sake of these sacred bones, a road has been made, with vast labor, up the mountain,

tain, which is of the hardeſt lime ſtone rock, and juſt not perpendicular. It is, with great propriety, called *La Scala,* or the ladder; and as the ſtones are quite deſtitute of ſoil, the aſcent is very dangerous as well as difficult. The proſpect from the top is beautiful and extenſive.

With the aſſiſtance of our indefatigably kind friend, Mr. Tough, we have this day made a bargain for a litiga and three ſaddle horſes, beſides one for our guard, and another for our baggage, to take us to Meſſina. The terms of the agreement have been drawn up by a public notary, and ſigned by each party. Bright and mild. N. E. Therm. at ſun riſe, 43.

TERMINI, *Feb.* 17.

HAVING already had a specimen of Sicilian accommodations in our journey to Segesta, and understanding that we were not likely to meet with much better fare in our road to Messina, we have provided ourselves with such additional articles as our absolute necessities require, and as the real wants of man are but few, an inventory of our furniture would make but a very mean figure in one of Christie's catalogues. It is as follows:

Kitchen.—A gridiron, ditto smaller, two stewpans, a toasting-fork, three knives, forks, and spoons, a tea-kettle, a chocolate-pot.

China-closet.—A tea-pot, three cups, two glasses.

Bed-chamber.—Three bags, a mattrass, one pair of sheets, one rug.

Add to this a piece of Irish beef, two tongues,

tongues, some Worcestershire perry, and a canister of hyson tea, with which we have been supplied by the liberality of Mr. Tough.

Having sent our litiga a little before us, we set out from Palermo in an open coach, which brought us as far as Bagaria, when we took to our litiga and saddle horses, since which we have travelled at the foot of mountains, by the sea side, and on a very good carriage road, to this town, which, though a poor place, is the largest I have *[seen?]* next to Palermo, and seems to be a*[l]*most entirely occupied by shoe-ma*[kers]*. In the neighbouring gardens ar*[e some]* very fine orange and lemon tree*[s;]* the country in general, through w*[hich]* we have past to-day, is uncultiva*[ted;]* and though the mountains are w*[ild]* and rocky, yet, being almost en*[tirely]* destitute of wood, they afford few picturesque scenes.

For Sicily we have found a tolerable inn, and our room has got a window. The provisions are unpacked, and the implements of cookery handseled. A frying-pan has been also wanted, and application made for one now hanging up in our landlord's kitchen. But here we have experienced the mortification of an absolute refusal; (it is meagre day) and this said frying-pan having been set apart for the purpose of dressing fish, must not be contaminated with the touch of any other kind of meat.

About two years ago a company of merchants in this town established a Society, for the purpose of robbing and murdering, most of whom have been

been taken up and hanged. Mr. Tough supped with one of them at this place, and as the gentleman appeared to be exceedingly agitated, frequently going out of the room, and returning again, Mr. T. is now perfuaded, that he was then engaged in his bloody occupation, and perhaps forming fome plan to take away his (Mr. T.'s) life. That perfon is among the executed. Mr. T. advifed us to place our guards and fervants, with fire-arms, at our chamber door whilft we flept, but this precaution we thought unneceffary, for we apprehended no danger, and happily found none. A quarrel took place as we came along, between our guide and a fifherman, and I verily believe the former would have fhot the latter, if his horfe had not run away with him in the critical moment that his

paffion

paſſion was at its height: for he primed, cocked, and preſented his gun, but having looſed his horſe's bridle, the beaſt ſet off, and did not give him time to diſcharge it. Warm. Thin clouds. S. E.

CEFALU, *Feb.* 18.

WE have had another day's journey of twenty-four miles. The carriage road ends at Termini, though it has been marked out a few leagues farther. We continued near the ſea, and forded four rivers, two of which were pretty conſiderable, without any intereſting proſpect, till we came within five miles of this town; when we found the mountains cultivated to their ſummits with large olives, feathering or rather bending

bending to the ground, intermixed with extenfive plantations of the manna afh, and fome fruit trees in full bloffom. The road is rough and ftony, over rocky mounds covered with evergreen fhrubs, and ornamented with a few neat houfes. This is a fmall town, confifting of feveral narrow dirty ftreets, fituated at the foot of a great rock, upon which is erected a caftle, only acceffible by a very narrow pafs, where it is defended by a ftrong wall; I fhould apprehend that the place obtained its name from the Greek word Κεφαλη, which fignifies a head or promontory. Our inn is tolerably clean, but it is without windows, without food, and without a fingle article of kitchen furniture; neverthelefs over the door is written *Pofata & Taverna,* Inn and Tavern. Mild, partly cloudy, and one flight fhower. S.E. and N.W.

STEFANO,

STEFANO, *Feb.* 19.

SUCH roads by such precipices I hope never to go again in any kind of vehicle. We were sometimes upon the sea-shore among great loose stones, and sometimes in narrow paths, oftener in no paths at all, on the sides of steep mountains, where one false step would probably have tumbled us down into the vast ocean beneath us. From these altitudes the Lipari Islands presented themselves to view, particularly Stromboli, in which is a volcano that burns continually. It appears to us like a great cone, with a crater at the top, from whence we saw immense columns of smoke ascending. These islands ship off annually 7000 barrels of raisins, and a large quantity of currants, which are made from a small black grape. At the distance of eighteen miles

miles from Cefalu we ſtopt to dine at a paltry village, and as our *ſalle a manger* was expoſed to public view, the country people had an opportunity, which they readily embraced, of ſeeing the lions, and how Engliſhmen eat and drink. We had only ſix miles further to compleat our day's journey, and are now at another little town. Here we flattered ourſelves with hopes of better accommodations, and expected the form of a viſit from the governor, to whom a letter had been written from Cefalu, praying him to procure us three beds. He has ſo far complied with our requeſt, as to order the beſt that the hole called an inn can furniſh, to be got in readineſs; but theſe are ſo bad, that we ſhall order our bags to be filled with ſtraw, and as uſual, lay down in our cloaths. The evening is cold, and I could enjoy a fire; but inſtead

ſtead of this, till we can purchaſe a little wood or charcoal, I am obliged to ſit at an open window, in a ſtrong current of air that blows my papers all about. Not one article of furniture of any kind in the houſe, except cobweb hangings, much leſs any thing to eat or drink, and no inhabitants but rats, mice, ſpiders, fleas, with ſome *et cetera*; the landlord and landlady, if ſuch there be, living elſewhere.

BROLO, *Feb.* 20.

A VARIETY of cauſes contributed to make us rejoice at the thoughts of leaving Stefano. The dogs barked inceſſantly for ſome hours, the cocks crowed, the aſſes brayed, and about midnight there was a violent cry of murder

murder juft under our window. Our Italian fervant anfwered the call, upon which the complainant ran away, and in the morning nobody could tell what had happened. Having no covering but a thin great coat, and a dreffing gown about my legs, I lay cold and fleeplefs till four o'clock in the morning, when I jumped up from my ftraw mattrafs, ready dreffed for the journey of the prefent day. Though commanded by our muleteers to rife fo early, we did not fet out till half paft fix, and travelled our firft ftage of twenty-one miles along a good Sicilian road, or rather a good road for Sicily, chiefly by the fide of uncultivated mountains, through thickets of myrtles, pomegranates, ciftufes, and a variety of other evergreen fhrubs. We ftopt to bait at a pleafant village, where there are two or three handfome palm-trees,

trees, and have since made another stage of twenty-one miles through a more cultivated country, producing corn, mulberries, and olives. Several towns are placed on the tops of the hills, and many villages on the plain below. From an high cape about five miles diftance we obtained a very fine view of the Lipari Iflands, and from thence have continued our courfe by the fide of a precipice, along a bold rocky fhore tolerably well wooded, and formed into inclofures for corn or vines. Our inn here is really worfe than that we got laft night, or any we have yet met with; hitherto we have generally been able to procure one or two hard mattraffes, though we feldom chofe to make ufe of them, on account of their filthinefs; but here is nothing of the kind, nor any fort of houfe-hold utenfil whatever; we have, how-ever,

ever, got three chairs since our arrival, and made a table by placing a board upon two baskets. Upon this table we are preparing to regale ourselves with some pork steaks which we brought with us, having made a fire in the middle of the room to cook them, upon our own useful gridiron. Good bread we get almost every where, the Sicilian corn being very excellent; also plenty of fresh macaroni, which is made in almost every little town in the island, and which our servants prepare for us in a few minutes, by boiling it in water, and grating upon it some parmesan cheese, a piece of which we always carry with us, as it may be had in any of the principal towns. For our chief refreshment, however, we are indebted to our tea and chocolate, though the former of these articles begins to run low, and I fear we shall not

not be able to buy any more till our return to Naples, this herb being almoſt unknown in Sicily, and never given but as a medicine. Butter there is none at all to be had, and no milk but that of ſheep or goats. Fiſh both ſalt and freſh, particularly anchovies, we have been able to procure at moſt places, and a very large ſort of ſprat, called *ſardelle*, which are very excellent when juſt taken; ſo that inſtead of regretting our bad fare, we have great reaſon to be thankful for many a good meal, eſpecially when we have had a ſlice of plumb pudding *pour la bonne bouche*, which our Engliſh ſervant made very well whenever we could get materials. High wind all morning, chiefly bright. Thermometer at 1, 62. Hot gleams in the evening, with wind and calms alternately. Thermometer at 3, 74. S.

BARCE-

BARCELONETTA, *Feb.* 21.

I REMEMBER reading some time ago of an officer, who, after the fatigue of an engagement, laid himself down upon the ground, and slept soundly, whilst the cannon balls were whizzing about his ears; I did not at that time credit the account, but I believe now that I could sleep under similar circumstances, as I was last night stretched upon my bag of straw, ere the supper was removed, and the other beds prepared, and was in a few minutes totally insensible to the clatter of four persons walking about the room, and every now and then jogging or stumbling over me, at the same time that a very tempestuous wind threatened our habitation with destruction. Four hours afterwards, I was called upon to hear a clap of thunder, rolling just over our heads,

heads, a second soon followed, and, as as I was told this morning, some more, but my inclination to sleep still continued, and I took another comfortable nap till half past five, when I was rouzed to pursue my journey. We first travelled under rocks, and then along a narrow road by the mountain side, where the precipices were exceedingly tremendous; in this part were large masses of stone, that appeared to contain many particles of silver, and glittered beautifully as the sun shone upon them. In descending the hill, we were agreeably entertained, with a tune upon the bag-pipes, played by a shepherd with much taste and execution, whilst the flocks of this Corydon were feeding all around him. About noon we arrived at our baiting place, (twenty-one miles) and dined in the stable. Our evening's ride, nine miles more, has

has been very pleasant. The mountains are lower, and flope eafily into a plain, a mile in width, cultivated with corn, vines, and mulberries, and backed by large groves of olive-trees. Several towns, villages, and detached houfes, contribute to the beauty of the landfcape. We obferved, that one fmall village was entirely new, and upon inquiring into the reafon of it, were informed, that the inhabitants of a neighbouring mountain, had been fo terrified by repeated earthquakes, that they were obliged to leave their old habitations, and in confideration of the loffes they had fuftained, were exempted from the payment of all taxes for ten years. We are come to a confiderable town, in which there is a manufactory of coarfe earthenware, and have taken up our lodging at a *princely* inn, the fign of the eagle, where we have a room ten feet square, in which are two beds, four chairs, a table, two shelves, and a wash-hand bason: There is, however, nothing at all in the house, either to eat or drink, nor so much as a bit of fuel for our servants to cook our victuals, without sending out to purchase it. I perceive little difference between the Sicilian and Neapolitan people. The women in these parts dress their heads in a very simple manner, with a ribbon bound round them, and tied in a bow at the top. The most remarkable part of the men's dress is their shoes, which may be made in about ten minutes, as they consist only of a piece of calf or goat's skin, just covering the heels and toes, and fastened by a string, which being wound round the leg, binds on a kind of buskin, made of coarse cloth. Cool and windy, 55.

Messina, *Feb.* 23.

Barcelonetta is situated among orchards of orange and lemon-trees, the fruit of which is so plentiful, that many lemons lie quite unheeded in the streets. The first eighteen miles of our road this morning, afforded delightful views of the same kind of scenery, as that we enjoyed yesterday, but more picturesque. The back ground is very wild, and the hills in one part, seem as if they had boiled up and congealed in the moment of ebullition. A few miles to the left, we saw the town of Milazzo, fortified with a new citadel, and embellished with many handsome buildings. It is in a singular situation, upon a promontory, which is at the same time a peninsula, being only connected to the main land by a very narrow slip of earth, little above the level of the sea.

sea. The house where we baited, belonged to the prince of Villa Franca, who perished in the earthquake of 1783. His palace, which we saw upon a mountain, stood the shock, but was seen to move up and down with a kind of undulatory motion. Our afternoon's ride has been twelve miles. Turning our backs upon the sea, we had a very curious road for three miles up the bed of a river, from whence we ascended an high mountain, mostly barren, remarking in our way the ravages of the earthquake, in the destruction of several cottages, as also many fissures in the ground, occasioned by the same terrible convulsion. The view of Messina with its grand harbor and ships from the top of this mountain, the straits and the high woody coast of Calabria with a considerable number of towns and villages, affords a *coup d'œil*, the finest that

that it is poffible to imagine. We defcended about three miles to the town. The environs are populous, and have been much more fo. The diffolution here appears to have been univerfal; many new and handfome houfes have been erected; but the majority of the inhabitants live in barracks, of one ftory high, without the walls. Such is our inn, *Il Leone d'oro*, the beft I have feen in this ifland, and the landlord a civil, obliging man. Mild. Th. 59. W. We obferved to day, oats in ear, and flax and lupins in flower. The latter are cultivated in great quantities in Sicily and Italy, for the purpofe of feeding the cattle; but the poor people often eat them, for want of better provifion.

MESSINA, *Feb.* 23.

PREVIOUS to our going to bed laſt night, the maſter of the inn told us, with great unconcern, that we might repoſe ourſelves in tranquillity, as the houſe was built with canes, and would either ſtand the ſhock of an earthquake, or ſuffer us to eſcape without much injury, in caſe of its demolition. We enquired how long it had been ſince the laſt ſhock, " three days " ago," (ſaid the landlord); " no, five," (ſaid the waiter). So little do theſe people regard what in England, or any other country, where earthquakes are leſs frequent, would be remarked with the moſt minute exactneſs. They have commonly three or four ſhocks every month, " ſome little and ſome great," as our landlord alſo obſerved; but the people in general have now ſurvived ſo many, that they ſpeak of them with the

the utmoſt indifference. The moſt conſiderate are, indeed, fearful of a more ſerious repetition of the former calamity, and anxiouſly wiſh for an eruption of mount Etna, to give vent to the ſubterraneous fires. Nothing can be more melancholy than the view of this once magnificent city now lying in ruins. The quay, which is the ſegment of a circle, a mile and a quarter in length, preſents the ruin'd fronts of a range of grand palaces, built of white ſtone, which were formerly four ſtories high, adorned with all the orders of coſtly architecture. Not one remains entire, the two upper ſtories being thrown down throughout.

Churches, palaces, and private houſes are all in the ſame condition in every part of the city. A new town is riſing out of the ruins of the old one, and it is is surprising to see how many magnificent houses have been already erected.

The Messinese writers inform us, that their city was founded near four thousand years ago, endowed from time to time with peculiar privileges, and notwithstanding some calamities, to which it has been subject *, raised in the present age to an high degree of beauty and magnificence. Among its ancient privileges one is mentioned as particularly worthy of observation, viz. That the Virgin Mary, upon the application of St. Paul, wrote an invaluable letter to Messina, filled with the most tender and affectionate expressions, whereby

* About the year 1670, the Messinese rebelled against the government, and sought the protection of Louis XIV. who abandoned them to the vengeance of the Spaniards: eighteen thousand persons left the city upon this occasion; it was deprived of many of its privileges, and, of course, fell into declension for some years. In 1743, the plague made such dreadful ravages, that 30,000 persons died in one day.

she declared herself to be the perpetual protectress of the city. To this was attributed its safety for many ages, while Palermo, Catania, and other cities of Sicily were overthrown or injured by terrible and repeated earthquakes. But (as the historian relates) the citizens having neglected to pay due adoration to the sacred virgin, she withdrew her protection, and the fair city of Messina became, in its turn, devoted to destruction. I shall relate the particulars of this calamitous event in the words of one who was a spectator of the dreadful scene.

" On the fifth day of the present
" February, (1783) an unpropitious
" day, and ever to be had in remem-
" brance by the beautiful Messina, about
" forty-eight minutes past eleven in
" the morning, the earth began to
" shake

" shake, at first slightly, then with
" such force, such bellowing, and with
" such various and irregular shocks,
" that the motion was similar to the
" rolling of the sea[*]. The walls
" gave way on every side, knocked
" together, and crumbled to pieces;
" the roofs were tost into the air, the
" floors shattered, the vaults broken,
" and the strongest arches divided. By
" the force of three or four shocks,
" which succeeded each other without
" a moment's intermission, many houses
" were reduced to ruin, many palaces
" thrown down, and churches and
" steeples levelled with the ground.
" At the same time a long fissure was
" made in the earth upon the quay,

[*] From this motion many persons were seized with giddiness and vomiting, and the very birds were so affected, that they suffered themselves to be taken by the hand.

" and

" and in an adjoining hill, while ano-
" ther part of the coaft was covered
" by waves. At that inftant a vaft
" cloud like afhes rofe furioufly from
" the horizon in the north-weft,
" reached the zenith, and defcended
" in the oppofite quarter. It grew
" darker at the moment of the con-
" cuffion, extended its dimenfions, and
" almoft obfcured the whole hemif-
" phere *. At the fame time alfo ap-
" peared upon the tops of the houfes
" and palaces that were falling to
" pieces, a fudden and tranfient flame,
" like thofe lightnings that glance
" from the fummer clouds, leaving
" behind it a fulphureous fmell †.

* The fame phenomenon was obferved in three fucceeding fhocks, that compleated the deftruction of the
city.

† The fame was feen in feveral parts of Calabria, and
has likewife been remarked in former earthquakes.

" The

" The wretched inhabitants now
" left their houfes in the greateft ter-
" ror and confufion, calling upon God
" with piteous cries for fuccour, and
" running to and fro about the ftreets,
" not knowing whither they fhould
" flee. In the mean while the build-
" ings on each fide were falling upon
" them, and the earth almoft conti-
" nually trembling under their feet,
" fo that in the fhort fpace of three
" minutes they were almoft all col-
" lected together in the fquares and
" open places of the city under the
" dreadful apprehenfions of inftant
" death. Every eye was bathed with
" tears, and every heart palpitated
" with fear, while they experienced an
" addition to their mifery, by being
" expofed to the violence of a tem-
" peftuous wind, attended with tor-
" rents of hail and rain. It is impof-
                              " fible

"fible for the pencil of the moft in-
"genious painter to delineate, or for
"the pen of the moft able writer to
"defcribe the horror and confufion of
"thefe wretched people. Each one
"fought for fafety in flight, and many
"in feeking it met with death. Others
"were buried alive under the falling
"houfes *, others hung upon the
"beams, others upon the threfholds
"of the windows and balconies, from
"whence by means of ropes and lad-
"ders they with difficulty efcaped with
"their lives, and others miferably pe-
"rifhed, either under the ftones and
"rubbifh of their own dwellings, or
"from the buildings, which fell upon
"them as they paffed through the
"ftreets.

* Rofa Santangelo, aged ninety-feven, was dug out of the ruins at Catania, in the year 1693. She was again buried by this earthquake at Meffina, and again preferved alive.

"They

"They who escaped unhurt, spent
"the rest of the day in preparing a
"place of shelter against the approach-
"ing night. Some little ill-built ca-
"bins, composed of furniture taken
"from the ruins, were raised in
"the space of a few hours, within
"which they lay together in promis-
"cuous companies upon the bare
"ground.

"The earth in the mean time con-
"tinued to shake incessantly, with a
"noise similar to a furious cannonad-
"ing, which seemed to proceed from
"within its bowels. Sometimes the
"shocks were weak, sometimes strong,
"and so continued till midnight, when
"with a most tremendous noise the
"shaking assumed a redoubled fury,
"and threw down all those edifices
"that had resisted the former shocks.
"Then

"Then fell part of the walls of the cathedral, the magnificent steeple, two hundred and twenty-five palms in height, part of the great hospital, the seminary of the priests, the remainder of the student's college*, the front of the palaces upon the quay, many churches, convents and monasteries, together with multitudes of private houses. At the same time the sea rose with an extraordinary roaring to a vast height, overflowed a long tract of land near a little lake called *Il Pantanello*, and carried back with it some poor cottages that were there erected, together with all the men, animals and vessels it met with in its passage, leaving upon the land, which had

---

* The greater part of the students, who had been immured by the falling of the buildings at the first shock, were now set at liberty, and escaped unhurt.

"been

" been overthrown, a great quantity
" of fish of various kinds.

" From twelve o'clock of the afore-
" said fifth of February to the mid-
" night following, the shocks were so
" frequent, that they succeeded each
" other without any interval longer
" than fifteen minutes, and continued
" much in the same manner till about
" three o'clock on the evening of the
" seventh, when the whole mine was
" sprung at once, and the last stroke
" given to the already ruined Messina.
" A cloud of dust that darkened the
" air rose from the falling city, and in
" this, more than in any of the former
" earthquakes, was felt a variety of mo-
" tions undulatory, vertical, &c. which
" shattered the walls to pieces, destroy-
" ed many buildings from their very
" foundations, and, as if pounded in

" a mortar, spread them over the sur-
" face of the earth *."

" Some few edifices that were found-
" ed upon rocks in the upper part of the
" city, are still standing, but they are
" for the most part so cracked and da-
" maged, that it is dangerous to go
" near them."

But, however terrible the earthquakes were at Messina, they were much more so in Calabria, where mountains were changed into vallies, and vallies into mountains, rivers turned, lakes formed, and the whole face of the country visibly altered.

* The whole number of persons that lost their lives at Messina, amounted to six hundred and seventeen, besides which, many others were wounded in a terrible manner. Two children, a boy and a girl, continued seven days under the ruins, and were then found alive, and it is reported of another, that he recovered after having been confined a still longer time. Some guinea-fowls subsisted without food seventeen days, and two mules twenty-four.

In a place called *Il lago del Monte*, about a mile from Seminara, a cottage with an adjoining orangery, and a man upon it, were carried to the diſtance of a mile.

In the diſtrict of Coſoleto, a large plain called Cineti ſunk above three hundred palms, and formed a deep valley, and a cottage was removed two gun-ſhots above its former ſituation, without receiving any injury.

In St. Criſtina, a vineyard ſituated upon an eminence, and a plantation of olives upon a plain, together with a tower erected upon it, changed places, ſo that the vineyard was upon a plain, and the plantation of olives upon an eminence, with the tower ſtanding as before. In the ſame diſtrict ſome per-ſons ſunk into a chaſm, which opened
under

under their feet, and were immediately thrown out again without receiving any material hurt; while others, who were travelling on horfe-back, were thrown from their feats and buried in the abyfs. In Soriano, two mountains were united, thirteen perfons were killed, and a large lake formed.

In a plain between Seminara and Le Pietre Negre, there appeared an hot lake throwing up its waters into the air. In the territory of Setizano, a large portion of land was joined to another belonging to Cofoleto, by means of which the courfe of a river was ftopped, and the country laid under water, for the fpace of feveral miles. A mountain above Sinopoli was torn from its centre, and carried acrofs a valley to the diftance of a mile and half. But the moft extraordinary circumftance hap-

happened to a Greek ship near the island of Lipari, which either sunk, or seemed to sink, from the waves being thrown up very high on each side, into the depths of the sea, and which recovered its former situation, not only without damage, but without receiving a drop of water in its inside.

The most violent force of the shocks, was extended through a tract of country fifty-eight miles long, and twenty broad, including a space of eleven hundred and sixty square miles.

When the astonishing effects of this, and former earthquakes in these parts * are

---

* Diod. Sic. Strabo, Virg. and other authors of credit, affirm, that in times immemorial the coast of Italy was separated from that of Sicily.

are duly confidered, the tradition which Plato received in Egypt, of the feparation of the American continent, by a convulfion of a fimilar nature, will appear much lefs improbable, than thofe

In the year 326, many cities in Sicily were greatly injured, Nicea deftroyed, and Conftantinople partly ruined.

In 1169, Catania was fo totally overthrown, that one ftone was not left upon another, and 15,000 perfons killed. All Sicily and Calabria felt the fhock, and received confiderable damage.

In 1456, all Calabria and Naples felt fhocks of uncommon violence.

In 1494, 1498, and 1509, Meffina fuffered much, and Reggio was deftroyed: 1542 is noted for an earthquake, that deftroyed Catania, Augufta, Noto, Callagerone, Militello, Palermo, Trapani, and many other cities. In 1566, Randazzo was deftroyed, and in 1570, all Europe was fhaken. In 1609, the city of Naples was reduced to ruins, and greatly injured in 1638, and immenfe damage done in both the Calabrias.—The fame city was again laid wafte in 1688, and in January 11, 1693, the whole ifland of Sicily was fhaken, with the death of 60,000 perfons. To thefe fucceeded other ftrong fhocks, in 1743-47-69 and 80, with many others of fmaller note.

who have never paid attention to the phænomena of earthquakes, are apt to confider it. For who can fet bounds either to the extent or force of thefe concuffions? Vefuvius, Stromboli, Etna, and Mount Semo, in Ethiopia, at leaft two thoufand miles diftant from the former, are faid to correfpond in their eruptions *.—If fo, there is certainly a

* Jones's Phyfiological Difquifitions.—The fame ingenious author fpeaking upon this fubject, fays, " This, " i. e. the feparation of America, is farther confirmed by " the prefent ftate of the intermediate iflands of the " Atlantic, the Canaries, Azores, &c. which appear " like fragments of a fhattered land, and bear the marks " of volcanoes and earthquakes in all parts of them, the " Pico Teneriffe itfelf, by the materials of which it is " compofed, being no other than an huge monument of " fome violent eruption. The fea, in which thefe " iflands are found, is ftill fubject to fubterraneous fires " rifing from its bottom, of which there have been recent " inftances, near the ifland Tercera, defcribed in the " Philofophical Tranfactions.

" In the year 1757, and in the month of July, all the " Azores fuffered greatly by an earthquake; eighteen " new iflands appeared, and confiderable tracts of the old " ones were fwallowed up."

con-

connection between them by subterraneous canals under the bed of the sea. But take away these vents, confine the volcanic matter within its original caverns, and then when the superincumbent strata of the earth have not sufficient strength to resist the force within, they will yield with a disruption vast as the Atlantic Ocean.

I shall close this account of earthquakes, with mentioning some of those phænomena, by which they are usually preceded or followed, and which it is of the utmost importance to the inhabitants of this country to consider with attention, that they may be able to escape the direful effects of an approaching shock.

From the fatal fifth of January, 1783, to the end of July, almost all the

the shocks (which, besides sixty-two in the first twenty-four hours, amounted to near one hundred) were preceded by a long streak of clouds, near the horizon, extending from the east to the south, which grew darker after sun-set, and were soon confounded with the other clouds *. In the course of the same year, particularly in the month of July, there was an extraordinary appearance of the Aurora Borealis, and such terrible thunder and lightning as was never before known; a few days after a globe of fire, a foot in diameter, was observed slowly moving through the air, between the south and south-east, leaving behind it luminous particles similar to those meteors, vulgarly called falling stars, which

* The same was remarked in the year 1693 and in 1780.

also

alſo were ſeen every evening in great quantities.

The ſun generally appeared obſcured by a miſt which ſpread itſelf ſo thickly in the lower regions of the atmoſphere, as to obſtruct the view of the Calabrian coaſt. The moon, at night, was in like manner darkened, or ſurrounded by an halo: it muſt, however, be obſerved, that on the days when this miſt was thickeſt, no ſhock was ever felt.

The winds were variable and inconſtant, except at the time of a ſhock; when there was a dead calm; but as ſoon as it was over, they ſprang up again, and in the ſpace of twenty-four hours, would change to every point in the compaſs.

The

The sea frequently rose higher than usual, with an uncommon roaring noise, and the wells at the same time became thick and turbid; a sure indication that an earthquake would follow in a few hours afterwards; and as the last signal, which only took place a few seconds before, Volcano and Stromboli cast up dense globes of smoke, very different from what was observed at other times.

The brute creation gave manifest indications of some extraordinary revolution, particularly before the great shock which happened on the seventh of February. Some oxen that were feeding in a meadow near Messina, placed their feet strongly against the earth, as if to oppose a force from beneath, and raising their heads into the air, bellowed with all their strength.

The

The birds fled about in a confused manner, and seemed afraid to perch upon the trees, or light upon the ground, and immense quantities of sea-geese were seen swimming upon the waters of the Faro.

A small fish, called Cicinello, esteemed a very great delicacy, was so plentiful at this time in all the Sicilian seas, that the fishermen were unable to find purchasers. An unusual quantity of other fish were also taken at this time on the western side of the island, whither they seemed to have retired from an apprehension of impending danger.

WE have with no small pleasure dismissed our muleteers, who are the greatest villains I ever had the misfortune to be in company with; every fowl,

fowl, lamb or kid they could feize unnoticed upon the road, were fnatched up and flain without mercy, and many that efcaped are ftill fenfible of the blows they received. The poor laborious mules got many a fevere ftroke, and dogs, cats and pigs ran groaning from the cruelty of thefe brutal Palermians. They expected our approbation for every ingenious act of roguery, and could hardly believe their cruelty to the beafts was not extremely acceptable. Cloudy and cool. Rainy evening.

MESSINA, *Feb.* 24.

THE front of the great church which withftood the force of the earthquake, is a fingular and beautiful piece of architecture. The portal is of white marble,

marble, ornamented with several figures, though it is difficult to say whether some that are represented climbing up vine-trees are intended for children, monkeys or angels. The ground of the wall is chiefly red, with compartments of Mosaic work in horizontal lines. At the end of the once magnificent quay is a public walk planted with poplars, which are just bursting into leaf; a curious slip of low land *, on which the barracks are erected, extends from thence, and forms the harbor. Rain continued till early this morning; cool fine day, and wet night.

* This land is in the shape of a sickle, or reaping hook, from whence Messina was formerly called by the Greeks *zancle,* who feigned that the sickle of Saturn fell upon this spot, and gave it its form. It was called Messina by the Romans, from *messis,* harvest.

GIARDINI,

GIARDINI, *Feb.* 25.

With fresh mules and fresh men, including two campieri, we set out this morning with an intention of visiting Catania and Syracuse. Our cattle are not so good as those we had from Palermo, nor our drivers so expert; but the experience of the day tells us they are honest and obliging. We travelled, as usual, by the sea-side, and for the first ten miles observed that almost every house had shared the fate of those in Messina.

Speaking of earthquakes, I should note before I leave the subject, that one happened three weeks ago in the Lower Calabria; which threw down seven houses, but the people escaped unhurt. It was likewise felt at Messina,

sina, and the ships in the harbor were thrown against one another with such violence, that many of them received considerable damage. Upon leaving the town, we passed through gardens, and then under beautiful marble rocks, variegated with red, white, green and brown. The country, like the rest of the island that we have already seen, is very mountainous, but there is, most of the way, a narrow plain by the sea, cultivated with corn, vines and mulberries. We were directed to take notice of a particular spot in one of the mountains, where there is a mine of silver, which is constantly guarded by a party of soldiers.

Fifteen miles on this side Messina there is not one house thrown down, though the shock was very sensibly felt. Our whole day's journey has been

been thirty miles, and the prospects very agreeable. We had a view of Etna most of the way; in the morning it was covered with clouds, but in the evening perfectly clear. It is now inacceſſible on account of the ſnow, and generally continues ſo till the month of June. The crater, which to us appeared but as a point, is four miles in circumference, and emits a ſmoke like Veſuvius and Stromboli. The latter mountain about two months ago diſcharged a ſtream of lava from its ſide near a village, and deſtroyed two hundred people.

We arrived at this place juſt after ſun-ſet, and were turned into a great cabin or hovel, with a fire on the floor, over which a pot was boiling, and the family ſitting round like the ſavages in the South-Seas, or the robbers

bers in Gil Blas. There was no chimney, and the walls were as black as jet. We were almoſt ſuffocated with ſmoak. Our banker at Meſſina, Signor Gregorio Faroe, who has ſhewn us very great civilities, and taken upon himſelf the trouble of providing every thing for our journey, charged one of our attendants with a letter to an eccleſiaſtic at this place, ſo that we only waited in the cabin till it was delivered. But the gentleman was not at home; however, we have obtained a pretty good chamber at another houſe, and ſince our coming into it have had a viſit from the benevolent prieſt, who has ſent us fruit and wine, offered us every thing that his houſe will afford, and made us promiſe to pay him a viſit upon our return. Fair and mild. Ther. 61.

CATANIA, *Feb.* 26.

BEING up early, we enjoyed the pleasure of seeing the sun rise out of the sea in a clear serene morning. Etna was then in full view, and received the rays upon its summit just four minutes before they reached us, as we stood upon the sea-shore. We had a delightful journey at the base of that great mountain whose lower region slopes into a fine plain, well cultivated, and well wooded; the almond trees, which grow here in great quantities, are almost all in full leaf, and beautifully ornamented with blossoms; there are likewise some fine groves of oaks, walnuts, figs, and olives, intermixt with corn-fields and vineyards. The barley is now coming into ear, and the flax and lupins are every where in flower.

For

For thefe laft twenty miles we have travelled over ftreams of old lava, which have extended even to this town, I fhould think full twenty miles from the crater. The people of the country believe Etna to be one of the mouths of hell, and that the devil has his ftation there, but that he sometimes pays a vifit to Vefuvius and Stromboli. They likewife affert, that every perfon who has attempted to gain the fummit, has been carried away in a whirlwind; but this ftory is as void of truth as the other; for the landlord of our inn, who generally attends ftrangers, told us that he had been at the top a hundred and twenty times *. He fays there is always a great rum-

---

* I have fince found that the accounts given by this gentleman do not deferve much credit; however, I believe he has been feveral times at the top of Etna, though not perhaps a hundred and twenty.

bling and commotion in the bowels of the mountain. The defcent to Catania through groves of fruit trees is highly beautiful; we faw the town at the bottom, and beyond a rich champaign country, which, after the wild fcenes we had paffed, was particularly agreeable. It is now the carnival, and many of the people are in mafquerade. Upon entering the town, we met a low phaeton and pair driven by two mafked poftilions abreaft in jackets and trowfers, with two perfons mafked within, and a mafked man in woman's cloaths ftanding behind. Bright and ferene, Ther. at one, 61.

CATANIA, *Feb.* 27.

THIS city has been deftroyed feven times, either by eruptions, or by earthquakes.

quakes. The laſt time was by an earthquake, in the year 1693. It is ſaid, that a century never elapſes without a calamity of this kind; if ſo, the preſent beautiful city muſt very ſoon be brought to deſtruction. The inhabitants, like thoſe in the vicinity of Veſuvius, apply to their tutelary ſaint in every time of danger. St. Agatha is the protectreſs here, and has, in common with the reſt in the popiſh calendar, a day ſet apart to her honor every year. Her veil is then thrown into the fire, and by a miracle comes out unburnt; but if it be made of aſbeſtos, (as I ſuppoſe it is) it would be a miracle indeed if it happened otherwiſe. When the city was laſt deſtroyed, the people that had time to eſcape lived upwards of thirty years in barracks, ſo that the preſent town is of more modern date than ſome of its inhabitants. The streets are perfectly straight, wide, and well paved with broad, flat stones, of lava. Many of the houses are magnificent, and the poorer ones have an air of neatness, but by far the greater part of each are built with lava. The churches are large, in an handsome style of architecture, but not much ornamented within, excepting one that has received a temporary decoration in honor of St. Agatha. The pillars and arches are covered with looking-glasses in silver frames, and between each pillar is a curtain of blue and pink, laced with silver. We took a walk this morning in a garden (if such it may be called) belonging to the prince of Biscari. Among mountains of lava are broad walks, wide enough for a carriage, and here and there a little grass and a few Indian figs growing through the cre-

vices

vices of the cinders. In the lower part is a fish-pond, fenced from the sea by a terrace of lava, a great part of which was thrown down by the earthquake of 1783. Near the water is one handsome palm-tree. This lava was from the last great eruption ninety-eight years ago. It caused the sea to retire near a mile from its ancient boundary, and from the height it now remains above the surface of the water, I may safely conjecture that it is at least thirty feet in thickness *. A fort-

---

* Sir William Hamilton, who surveyed mount Etna with great accuracy in 1769, relates, that in the great eruption of 1669, by the stones and cinders alone, a hill was formed one mile in height, and three in circumference; and that the stream of lava was fourteen miles long; in many places six wide, and fifty feet in thickness. This eruption did not proceed from the crater at the top of the mountain, but broke out near the base, as indeed the eruptions have generally done for some centuries past, the boiling matter being unable to rise to so great a height as twelve or thirteen thousand feet.

refs that stood by the walls of the old town remains, without injury, in its original situation. In a room belonging to the cathedral there is a large picture, very coarsely executed, representing the city and the stream of liquid fire that flowed by its walls, with an inscription at the bottom, signifying that what the lava spared, the earthquake destroyed. Mr. Brydone, in the history which he gives of this wonderful mountain, insinuates, that it is of much greater antiquity than the world itself, according to the Mosaic account. As a proof of this bold conjecture, he observes, vol. i. p. 124, 125, that a stream of lava which flowed two thousand years ago, is " as " yet only covered with a very scanty " vegetation ;" and concluding that the vegetative procefs is always similar, dates the age of the mountain according

ing to the various ſtrata of lava and ſoil that have been diſcovered. " Near
" a vault (ſays he) which is now
" thirty feet below ground, and has
" probably been a burial-place, there
" is a draw-well, where there are ſe-
" veral ſtrata of lavas, with earth to
" a conſiderable thickneſs over the
" ſurface of each ſtratum. Recupero
" has made uſe of this as an argu-
" ment to prove the great antiquity of
" the eruptions of his mountain: for
" if it requires two thouſand years or
" upwards to form but a ſcanty ſoil on
" the ſurface of a lava, there muſt
" have been more than that ſpace of
" time betwixt each of the eruptions
" which have formed theſe ſtrata.
" But what ſhall we ſay of a pit they
" ſunk near to Iaci of a great depth?
" They pierced through ſeven diſtinct
" lavas, one under the other, the ſur-
" faces

"faces of which were parallel, and
"moſt of them covered with a thick
"bed of rich earth. Now (ſays he)
"the eruption which formed the
"loweſt of theſe lavas, if we may be
"allowed to reaſon from analogy,
"muſt have flowed from the moun-
"tain at leaſt fourteen thouſand years
"ago."

As I have a much greater veneration for the writings of Moſes, confirmed by the teſtimony of the moſt ancient authors, of Chriſt and his apoſtles, and of the whole body of the Jewiſh nation, than for the teſtimony of one Sicilian author, plauſible as his account may appear, I muſt beg leave to make a few obſervations againſt this ſuppoſed antiquity of the mighty Etna.

In

In the first place, Mr. Brydone supposes Seignior Recupero, whom he calls "*the historiographer of Etna*," a very competent judge of the circumstances above related, and seems to take upon trust the greater part of what that volcanic philosopher has thought proper to advance. Admitting that gentleman to possess a very considerable share of knowledge, we may yet hazard a conjecture in supposing that his observations have been chiefly confined to the regions of Etna, and in that case he might possibly mistake other dark strata, in the well at Iaci, of whose nature he was unacquainted, for those of lava *. However, without calling in

---

* Near Viterbo there is a hill that seems to be composed of volcanic matter, though there are no other marks of any volcano in the neighbourhood. Indeed, the appearance of the hill itself, which is a low, long bank, is a sufficient proof that it was neither thrown up nor consists of lava run into that form.

queſtion either the veracity or the knowledge of the canonic· Recupero; Mr. Brydone himſelf furniſhes ſufficient matter to refute his own hypotheſis. " Our landlord at Nicoloſi,
" (ſays he) gave us an account of the
" ſingular fate of the beautiful coun-
" try near Hybla, at no great diſtance
" from hence. It was ſo celebrated
" for its fertility, and particularly for
" its honey, that it was called Mel.
" Paſſi, till it was overwhelmed by the
" lava of Etna ; and having then be-
" come totally barren, its name was
" changed by a kind of pun to Mal
" Paſſi. In a ſecond eruption, by a
" ſhower of aſhes from the mountain,
" *it ſoon re-aſſumed* its ancient beauty
" and fertility, and for many years
" was called Bel Paſſi." How ſoon ? I apprehend in a much ſhorter ſpace than two thouſand years; and as

Iaci

Iaci appears to be as near the mountain as Bel Paſſi, why may not ſome of the ſeven layers be fertilized by the ſame cauſe? Again, page 125, ſpeaking of the progreſs of vegetation, he ſays, " This progreſs, I ſuppoſe, is " *often* greatly accelerated by ſhowers " of aſhes from the mountain, as I " have obſerved in ſome places the " richeſt ſoil, to the depth of five " or ſix feet, and upwards; and ſtill " below that nothing but rocks of " lava." Speaking of a convent of Benedictine monks, p. 147, he writes, " Their garden is the greateſt curioſity: " although it be formed on the rugged " and barren ſurface of the lava, it " has a variety and neatneſs ſeldom to " be met with. The walks are broad " and paved with flints, and the trees " and hedges (which, by the bye, are " in a bad taſte, and cut into a num-
" ber

"ber of ridiculous fhapes) thrive ex-
"ceedingly. The whole foil muft have
"been brought from a great diftance,
"as the furface of this lava (*only one
"hundred and fifty years old*) is as hard
"and bare as a piece of iron." Why
might not foil have been brought to
cover former lavas as well as this? When it is confidered how extremely populous thefe parts were in former ages; it may be eafily fuppofed, that the people would ufe their utmoft induftry to refertilize the lands which the lava overflowed. If fuch an event can happen in fo fhort a fpace, I fee no reafon for rejecting the Mofaic regifter of the world's age.

But there is another objection yet unanfwered, we read, p. 189, 190, "I
"obferved, that this region of Etna,
"like the former, is compofed of lava;
"but

" but this is now covered so deep with
" earth, that it is no where to be seen
" but in the beds of the torrents. In
" many of these it is worn down by
" the water to the depth of fifty or
" sixty feet, and in one of them still
" considerably more. What an idea
" does not this give of the amazing
" antiquity of the eruptions of this
" mountain!" But is it extraordinary,
that a country so rent as this is by repeated earthquakes, should abound with deep chasms, through which the water would run as the most natural passage, without requiring ages *to wear itself away?* I did not particularly attend to this circumstance in my road, but I must have crossed all the streams that flow between the mountain and the sea, and do not remember one deep chasm all the way. There is indeed one considerable river that runs through a bed

of very ancient lava, which evidently appears to have been worn by the attrition of the water, but it is by no means fo deep as to require above two or 3000 years for the purpofe. All thefe circumftances taken together, I fhall remain an infidel to infidelity till ftronger evidence, againft the writings of Mofes be brought to light.

We had letters from Signor Joenai, the king's chamberlain at Naples, to his brother in this town, who has fhewn us a mufeum, containing the natural curiofities of Sicily, and fome of Vefuvius, excellently arranged according to the Linnæan method, in fome fmall elegant rooms fet apart for the purpofe. The chamberlain has found a new fpecies of cockle, fome of which have a place in the mufeum, under the name of Joenai. He has likewife publifhed lished a small pamphlet, containing a description of this wonderful shell. The small shells are placed in little glass boxes, each of which has a magnifier at the top. He shewed us the muscle, from the hair of which is made a kind of fine cloth.

The women of Catania, appear like mourners at a funeral, having long black cloaks that reach down to the ancles; they are neither made up, nor trimmed, and drawn so close over the face, that little more than the nose is visible.

We have been this evening with the Chevalier Joenai, to see the antiquities of the place. The first to which he conducted us is some feet below the level of the street, and appears to have shared the fate of Herculaneum, in being overwhelmed by a stream of lava. The purpose for which the building was erected is not certainly known. The part that has been excavated is strongly vaulted, and supported by nine square pillars of lava at equal distances. In several parts are discoverable some figures of plaister, or stucco, in good preservation, and extremely well wrought. From thence, we went to view some ancient baths, not long since discovered, by the prince of Biscari, who has examined into these monuments of antiquity with the most indefatigable labor. We afterwards took a view of the theatre, which still continues above ground, but is so surrounded and filled up by modern buildings, that without an excellent cicerone, we should have found much difficulty in tracing out its dimensions. It is somewhat larger than the theatre of

Mar-

Marcellus at Rome, which was three hundred and sixty-six feet in diameter, and able to contain upwards of 30,000 spectators. This theatre consisted of three stories, crowned by an attic, of which some vestiges are yet remaining.

A vast quantity of marble has been found in this spot, and among other marks of its ancient magnificence, were six granite pillars, which now stand in the cathedral. The prince of Biscari possesses the base of one of these pillars, which is admirably well preserved. This theatre was first erected by the Greeks, after which it fell into a ruinous state, and was restored by the Romans. Adjoining to this, has been discovered another theatre, much smaller, and built in a very simple style of architecture. We were next conducted to the amphitheatre, which was discovered likewise by the prince already mentioned, below the furface of the earth; its form is oval, like all other amphitheatres. One end refts againſt a mountain, and at the other is a wall conſtructed with maſſes of lava.

After feaſting our eyes with theſe antiquities, we were driven in the chevalier's coach feveral times through the fame ſtreets, every now and then ſtopping amidſt a crowd of carriages to fee and be feen; a fpecies of amuſement that the Sicilian and Neapolitan gentry are extremely fond of. As no kind of wheeled vehicle can go out of the town, on account of there being no roads, and as that is of no great magnitude, one would fuppofe that few carriages were kept, however, I was aſſured that there are at leaſt two hundred. The common people appear every afternoon in the moſt ridiculous mafquerade, and
the

the people of fashion have their masked balls at night, which continue till daybreak. Fine mild day, but not so bright as yesterday.

CATANIA, *Feb.* 28.

A SMART shock of an earthquake was felt here last Christmas-day, but the Catanians are not so subject to that calamity as the Messinese. The latter impute their frequent alarms to the present tranquillity of Etna, whereas the Catanians affirm, that if the ground about Messina has any connection with the subterraneous caverns of the mountain, the ground here should have a greater, and consequently be subject to greater agitations. But may not the phænomenon be explained upon this prin-

principle? The ground which is at the base of the mountain has so close a connection with it, that the common eruptions of smoke and flame give a vent to the sulphureous particles, whereas that which is more remote cannot be delivered from them but by more violent explosions.

The Chevalier Joenai has taken us in his uneasy vehicle to see a convent of Monks of the same order, and the same society as those at St. Martino; it is a large edifice containing an handsome library, a good museum, and a very large church in which is an exceeding fine organ. From thence we went to the museum of the prince of Biscari, containing a very capital collection of curiosities, such as busts, statues, inscriptions, fossils, minerals, animals, &c. &c. Among the fossils is a stony

mass,

mafs, inclofing the two jaws and teeth of fome animal, moft probably of a dog.

The nobility and gentry in Italy and Sicily affect a deal of ftate, and to make a figure in public place all the fervants they can mufter up behind their carriages. They are not, however, remarkably nice with refpect to their drefs and liveries, when they ftay at home. The fhoes of their domeftics are often all in holes, and their fhirts and ftockings coarfe, ragged, and filthy in the extreme. As we paffed through the great hall at the prince of Bifcari's, one of the fervants was charitably engaged in deftroying certain animals which abounded in the head of his comrade. Serene and mild.

AUGUSTA, *March* 1.

UPON obferving a fine plain from Catania, extending a confiderable way towards Syracufe, I anticipated a delightful

lightful day's journey, but have been much disappointed in finding a dead flat for the first twenty miles, with little tillage, and very few trees. The road by places extremely bad *. The last twelve miles were more agreeable. After ascending an hill planted with olives, we came to a rocky waste, which was soon contrasted by corn-fields and lawns, embellished with fruit-trees, palms, and cottages. Previous to our arrival in the town, our guards were ordered to lay down their arms. We entered by a strong fortress apparently new, were examined at the gates, and were conducted by a soldier with his musket in his hand to the guard-house, where

* When we had proceeded about ten miles from Catania, my brother, who had just quitted his litiga *for safety*, and mounted *Cocca-Sangue's Rosinante*, met with an accident, which might have been attended with very serious consequences. Whilst he was riding on a very narrow path, on a raised ridge of earth, the bank gave way, and he and his horse both tumbled into a pit of mud below; had he fallen half a yard farther, man and beast would probably have been suffocated, but providentially by the assistance at hand, both *the horse and the rider* were soon extricated from their difficulty, and neither of them received any other injury, but what a little mirth qualified, and pure water easily repaired.

we were interrogated by an officer that spoke English, and told us he was *an Irishman born at Augusta*. From him we were sent under the same guard to the commandant, who first addressed us in French, but upon learning our nation, he spoke to us in good English; he behaved with the greatest politeness, and offered his services in any manner that we chose to make use of them. He is a native of Cadiz in Spain.

We are lodged at a convent of Augustines, not sumptuously, but *comfortably* for Sicily, at least I *now* think so, though were I in England, I should probably esteem it a great hardship to lie upon a straw bed with no other furniture than a rug to cover me. On our account, the holy fathers have set aside their midnight or two o'clock prayers; which is, I believe, a *privilege* they

they are glad to enjoy when any strangers come to the convent.

The town is a tolerable one, and the streets wide and straight, though there are no fine buildings. It is situated upon a peninsula, which is now made an island by the fortifications, and the water that passes under the drawbridge. We have a magnificent view from this convent of a fine sloping shore as far as Syracuse, which being now covered with green corn, forms a beautiful lawn.

The greatest instance of distress I ever beheld, was exhibited this evening by a poor woman, who in purchasing some earthen ware from a Neapolitan vessel, had made a mistake of about two shillings in the change. She cryed, she roared, she stampt, and beat her

her breaſt with ſo much violence, that the blows might be heard to a conſiderable diſtance. All the arguments ſhe could uſe with the man, that ſhe thought had deceived her, only expoſed her to greater ridicule. My brother, who was a ſpectator of the poor creature's diſtreſs, told her he had found the money, and upon amply making up the loſs, ſhe fell upon the ground to kiſs his feet.

Upon quitting the convent we made the monks a preſent of about a guinea for our lodging, which, as they are a begging order, they readily accepted as a matter of charity, and ſaid they hoped to ſee us in our return.

Syracuse, *March* 2.

We crossed a gulph from Augusta in an open boat, and met our mules on the opposite side; from thence we travelled over a barren stony country, capable of cultivation, but at present only affording pasturage to a very few cattle. About four miles distant from this town, we ascended a very rough old pavement, called *Scala Græca**, and remarked that the rocks on each side had been worn into furrows by the wheels of carriages. The ancient roads branched off in a variety of directions, and as they were all worn in the same manner, the carriages must not only have been extremely numerous, but exceedingly heavy. Near the same place are some caverns, which our

---

* The Greek ladder.

guides informed us had been the habitations of the Greeks.

This town, so famous in history, has almost totally lost its former splendor, but is still rendered a place of note by its fortifications, which are almost new, and amazingly strong. We passed through five gates before we got into the town, and were examined at the first respecting our nation and business. Upon our arrival we went to what was called the inn, in which we had scarcely been five minutes, before we saw swarms of fleas creeping up our legs, which drove us hastily out of the house, and have, after a good deal of trouble, proved the means of getting us much better apartments. Warm, and some sun. Th. 61. S.E.

SYRACUSE,

SYRACUSE, *March* 3.

THE history of Syracuse is little known till the time of Gelon, (four hundred and eighty-five years before the birth of Christ) under whose mild and equitable government it acquired much of that strength which rendered it so formidable for many succeeding ages. Gelon bequeathed the dominion to his brother Hiero, and upon his decease to his brother Thrasibulus, who upon treating his subjects in a tyrannical manner, was deposed after a reign of only ten months. Upon this the citizens of Syracuse, and of the other cities who had groaned under the same yoke of servitude, were declared free, and in that state, upon an application from the Agrigentines, greatly increased their reputation in a successful war against the Siculi. Elated with victory,
they

they thought themselves in condition to give law to the whole island, and invaded the territory of the Leontines, who being reduced to great straits, invited the Athenians to their affiftance, who accordingly came over, ravaged the Æolian iflands, at that time in confederacy with Syracufe, defeated the Myleans as they were marching to join the Syracufans, took their city, and committed great devaftation in the enemy's country. As the Athenians continued to encreafe their forces, the Leontines were apprehenfive they meant to reduce the whole ifland, and therefore ftopt their career by concluding a feparate peace with the Syracufans, upon which they were made free of Syracufe.

It was about ten years after this that the Athenians had a frefh opportunity of attempting the reduction of the ifland, island, upon being invited over to the afsiſtance of the Egeſtans. The diſappointment they met with upon that expedition I have already mentioned, and their intention thereupon of turning their arms againſt this city. The ſiege was carried on with great vigor, and the loſs of the beſiegers and beſieged continued for ſome time nearly equal. At length, about the end of the third year, victory declared in favor of the Syracuſans, and out of forty thouſand Athenians that landed in Sicily, a very ſmall number returned to Greece, eighteen thouſand being ſlain in one engagement, beſides many more that were cut off in different ſkirmiſhes; ſix thouſand ſurrendered as priſoners of war, upon condition that their lives ſhould be granted them; but being reduced to ſlavery, and treated with great barbarity, moſt of them

them died of the hardships which they suffered.

The war with Carthage next succeeded, and was also occasioned by the Egestans, who, dreading the resentment of the Syracusans, and a fresh attack from the Selinuntines, invited that nation over to their assistance. The invitation was readily accepted, and Hannibal sent over with an army of three hundred thousand men.

Without entering into a particular detail of the sieges carried on, and battles fought by this enterprising people, suffice it to say, that after lavishing an immense treasure, and losing several hundred thousand brave men in attempting to reduce the island under their dominion, they were at last obliged to abandon it to the Romans, who, under the command of the Conful Marcellus, laid fiege to Syracufe, and took it at the end of three years. It was enabled to hold out fo long by the wonderful fkill of Archimedes the mathematician, whofe engines were conftructed in fo furprizing a manner, and did fo much execution on the befiegers, that the accounts hiftorians give of them appear almoft incredible.

When the place was taken, the Roman general treated the conquered with the greateft clemency, and exprefsly ordered his foldiers, while they feized the booty, to fpare the lives of the citizens. But this order was not fufficient to reftrain their fury; many perfons were put to death, and among the reft the great Archimedes. He was very calmly drawing his lines, when he faw a foldier enter his room, and

and put a fword to his throat. " Hold, friend, (faid he) one moment, and my demonftration will be finifhed." The foldier, aftonifhed at his unconcern, refolved to carry him to Marcellus; but Archimedes taking under his arm a fmall box full of mathematical inftruments, the foldier thought it contained a treafure; and not being able to refift the temptation, killed him upon the fpot.

Syracufe was founded by Archias, a Corinthian, upwards of feven hundred years before the birth of Chrift, and was, according to Strabo, one of the moft famous cities in the world for its advantageous fituation, the ftatelinefs of its buildings, and the immenfe wealth of its inhabitants: it was divided into four parts, diftinguifhed by the names of Acradina, Tyche, Neapolis and Ortygia, all of which were included within a treble wall twenty-two miles in compafs, and which was fo flanked with towers and caftles at proper diftances, that it was deemed impregnable. Acradina, which was the largeft part of the city, was fituated upon the fea-fide, and divided from Neapolis and Tyche by a wall of an extraordinary thicknefs and height. The fecond city called Tyche ftood between Acradina and an hill called Epipolæ, where there was a ftrong fortrefs, and feveral other buildings, infomuch that fome fpeak of it as a fifth city. The third city called Ortygia was built upon an ifland, and joined to the reft by a bridge; the fourth was called Neapolis, or the new city, becaufe built after the other three. There were two harbors near each other, being only feparated by the ifland; they were denominated

nominated the great and small, and both were surrounded by stately edifices.

SYRACUSE, *March* 3.

THE Baron Miloco, to whom we had letters from the governor of Catania, who resides at Messina, visited us this morning, and took us in his carriage to see the remains of this once magnificent city. The first object that engaged our attention, was a Grecian theatre situated upon an hill, about half a mile distant from the town, and which seems to defy all the ravages of time, being more than half formed by the natural situation of the ground, and having all its seats hewn out of the solid rock. Just above is an aqueduct,

partly

partly hewn, and partly built, and a little beyond, a fingular ftreet, cut through a rock, with a range of tombs on each fide. Near the fame fpot is a curious ftone quarry, in one part of which is a large cavern, called Dionyfius's car, becaufe it winds fomewhat in that form, and was turned into a prifon by that tyrant; it is eighty feet high, and one hundred and twenty long. An honeft miller, who labors on the ftream that ftill flows copioufly from the ruined aqueduct, attended us thither with an horn of powder, to amufe us with the echoes of that furprizing vault, but the experiment was very near producing fatal confequences, as the powder in the horn accidentally took fire. Providentially the quantity was very fmall, and no injury followed. No arguments could prevail with the man to accept any thing for his trouble,

ble, and for the ~~injury~~ loss he had sustained, though by his appearance, pecuniary assistance would have been very acceptable. In the center of the quarry is an high insulated rock, with a castle on the top, erected by the Saracens. Passing from thence over a few fields, we came to some small caverns, one of which is simply ornamented over the entrance, with Doric architecture cut in the solid rock. A little farther, we found a Gothic church under ground, said to be the first Christian one in the island *; it is very small,

---

* The sacred writings inform us, that the apostle Paul tarried here three days, after being shipwrecked on the neighbouring island of Malta or Melita, as it was anciently called. It is certain there were churches here very early, we read of them in the second and third centuries, and in the time of Constantine, at the beginning of the fourth century, there was a church in the city, of which Crestus was bishop, to whom the emperor wrote a letter himself, which is still extant in Eusebius. Had

the

small, and still used for the celebration of mass. Above is another church, or rather chapel, of modern date, adjoining to which stands an ancient Gothic wall, ornamented with an handsome window. From the lower church, we were conducted into the catacombs, which are said to extend as far as the ancient city, and are not less curious than those at Naples. After traversing a long passage, in the sides of which are niches for the dead, we came to a round hall, about twenty feet in diameter, and tapering like a cone to the top, which seems to have been formerly open. From the hall, are three or four passages, leading to other halls of the same kind, and so on through labyrinths, that no mortal has the cou-

the Christians in those days discovered the *amazing antiquity* of the Etna lava, they would hardly have suffered persecution for the cross of Christ.

rage

rage to explore. The tombs in the paffages are formed one behind another, and extend backwards into the rock, to the number of twenty-five in a row. The halls, it is fuppofed, were intended for families of diftinction. In the midft of fome is a large tomb for the chief, and around are cavities for the reft of the family. There are a few ornaments remaining, and one or two Greek infcriptions.

In the modern town, which is now confined to the ifland Ortygia, is a new church, made out of an old Grecian temple, dedicated to Mercury; fome of the pillars are antique, in the Tufcan ftyle. Of the fame kind are two others, now in the wall of a private houfe, but which formerly belonged to a temple of Venus.

In some conversation which we had with the baron, he informed us, that it was his intention to visit England next year, and desired to know whether we travelled upon camels, or by any more convenient mode of conveyance. He was not very well adapted for a Cicerone, for though a native of Syracuse, he had not visited the antiquities for several years, and never but once in his life; however, he procured us a juvenile antiquarian, who, by the assistance of the baron's brother-in-law acting as prompter, went through his part pretty well. The last of these gentlemen, who, in all other respects, seemed to be a man of sense and veracity, informed us, that the ice had been strong enough this winter to *bear an ox*, and was *a foot in thickness*. If he made no greater excursions from Syracuse than the baron, he might possibly

bly (not knowing the effects of a moderate frost) fancy all this the production of a cold morning. But such severity of weather is, without doubt, unknown in thirty-seven degrees of north latitude; certain I am, that in latitude thirty-eight, and that at Palermo, the ice in the severest part of the winter was never thicker than half a crown, and even that was reckoned very extraordinary, ice at Palermo being a sight as wonderful as an horse at Venice.

We took a walk after dinner to a convent of Capuchins, about a mile out of town, where there is one of the most uncommon and delicious gardens imaginable. It lies in a deep quarry, hewn into irregular forms, with rude arches of great dimensions, cut through in different parts. The rock is soft, and being worn away in several places,

ap-

appears almoſt natural. The area is filled with oranges, lemons, citrons, olives, pomegranates, vines, and almonds, all of which were planted by one monk, who died a few days before our arrival, aged eighty-ſix. Indian figs and ivy hang down from the top, and add much to the picturesque ſcenery of that romantic ſpot. By the ſea ſide the foundations of ancient buildings are eaſily to be diſcovered, and we found many fragments of Grecian earthenware mixed with the ſhells and pebbles upon the ſhore. The rocks contain various kinds of foſſils, of which there are great quantities in this iſland. Serene and warm; a little rain in the morning. Bright evening. E. S. E.

CATANIA,

CATANIA, *March* 4.

AFTER having afforded two good meals to a very flourishing colony of fleas, we left Syracuse at day-break, and, except passing the promontory on which Augusta is situated, and which is better cultivated than the neighbouring country, returned by the road we came. All things went so smoothly for the first sixteen or eighteen miles, that we very naturally entered into a conversation upon the *conveniences* of travelling in Sicily, and had just resolved to advise some of our friends who intended making the same tour, not to put themselves to the expence of engaging campieri, when one of our's turned sharply about and galloped full speed, to rescue the men who were behind with the baggage from an armed man on horseback, who had com-

commanded them to turn the mules back, and not to cry out upon pain of death. The robber, upon feeing our guard, rode off to two of his companions, who were waiting with guns at a little diftance.

We met with a fecond alarm, which might, in almoft any other fituation, have been attended with dangerous confequences; for as our cattle were trotting, which they fcarcely ever did, our carriage was thrown over into the fea, providentially upon the fand, where there was very little water, fo that we did not receive the fmalleft injury.

We arrived here a little after funfet, tired with our long journey (forty-fix miles) over the moft uncultivated part of Sicily. There is an hawthorn now in flower that feems to be of the
fame

same sort as the Glastenbury; and as this country is directly opposite the western side of Judea, it is *as reason-able* to suppose, that a seed was transported hither, as that Joseph of Arimathea's staff took root in England.

The lilies now in flower are various and beautiful. The most common sort grows to the height of three or four feet, and has many branches; the flower is white, streaked with purple down the middle of each leaf. Another, of which species I have seen one only, is white and small; and a third yellow, tipp'd with a bright glossy red on the three lower petals, which turn downwards in a curve. The blue iris is common, but much lower than in our gardens, as also the marygold, the purple blue anemone, and a large daisy with dark brown seeds, surrounded by a star a ſtar of bright red leaves. Theſe, and a few more, embelliſh the Sicilian plains in the depth of winter. Among the wild herbs is the aſparagus; but the plants are ſo ſlender, that in England we ſhould not judge them worthy of a place at our tables. There are ſugar-canes in the neighborhood of Syracuſe, and in ſome other parts of the iſland; but though they are ſaid to thrive well, the people take little pains to cultivate them, ſo that ſugar is no article of commerce with the Sicilians. The piſtachio nut, which grows on the ſouthern coaſts, turns to ſome profit. We were told at Palermo that this tree would not flouriſh upon that ſide the iſland, but our friend Mr. Tough ſays the experiment has been never tried. However, it is a known fact that one of theſe plants will never grow ſingle, but the male and female muſt ſtand

within

within a very small distance of each other. The leaf much resembles that of the common liburnum.

Near Syracuse are many stones, and some of them large, that appear to have been the production of a volcano; and if my information be right, there was one formerly about two miles from the city; a few years ago some acres of ground in the same neighborhood sunk down, I presume into one of the caverns produced by volcanic eruptions. Mild morning, evening cloudy and cold. Ther. 65. N.E.

MESSINA, *March* 6.

AT Catania is one of the best inns in all Sicily, *il Leone d'oro*. The landlord

lord of which, Don Lorenzo Abbate, (commonly known there by the name of *Cacca Sangue*) was our Cicerone to Syracuse, and was of some, though not much use. We travelled our former road yesterday over streams of ancient lava, and lay at a small town, where there is a great manufactory of macaroni. To our great surprize we found a clean comfortable house, where I ventured to trust myself in sheets, and passed the night unmolested by vermin.

This morning we rose before daybreak, and by that means got a view of the fire of Etna. It was a dim red light, like the sun in a thick fog, and seldom continued visible for two minutes together; though I am told it sometimes flames majestically, even when there is no eruption. It is impossible poffible to conceive any thing more tremendoufly noble than the appearance of this volcano, according to the poet's defcription:

―――Sed horrificis juxtà tonat Etna ruinis.
Interdumque atram prorumpit in æthera nubem,
Turbine fumantem piceo et candente favilla:
Attollitque globos flammarum, et fidera lambit:
Interdum fcopulos avulfaque vifcera montis
Erigit eructans, liquefactaque faxa fub auras,
Cum gemitu glomerat, fundoque exæftuat imo.
VIRG. ÆN. III. l. 571.

We paffed again by the village of Giardini, and ftopt at the door of the benevolent prieft, to thank him for his civilities; but as he was from home, a multitude of compliments were loft beyond redemption. Upon a mountain above is a confiderable town called Taormina, where there is an amphitheatre, and fome other antiquities; we did not go to the town, but faw the amphitheatre (of which there are but small remains) *en passant*, as the road lies a little below. We reached home (for such this place seems to be at present) about sun-set, and found several masquerade parties dancing in the street with as much festivity as if Messina were the most prosperous city in the universe, though the day after we left it, at two o'clock in the morning, there was so smart a shock of an earthquake, that a wooden saint was thrown down upon some candles which the people's devotion had lighted up in one of the churches, by which part of the inside was burnt. Even some of the inhabitants were much alarmed, and left their houses; but earthquakes being so common here, the people forget the danger as soon as it is over, and seem to imagine that frequent deliverances insure them from all future calamities.

The spring is forwarder here than at Syracuse, though nearly a degree farther north; and the buds of several trees, particularly the figs and poplars, are now expanding. Bright. Th. 63.

Messina, *March* 7.

The new houses in this town are built exceedingly strong, having the lower story constructed with arches, which are let for shops, and shut up by folding doors the whole size of the arch. In this part of the country are black and white asses, very handsomely variegated. A curious creature of the fish kind was exhibited here yesterday; it had a deep mouth, several rows of teeth, and four long tails. A kind of glue

glue was emitted from its body, by which it could attach itself to a man so strongly as to kill him. This fish I am told is eatable. The lobsters in these seas are remarkably good; they are nearly of a purple color, which they do not much change by boiling: their bodies are covered with little sharp prickles, which no doubt are a defence against fishes of prey, and they have no claws, at least I never saw one that had, though we have frequently bought them when just taken out of the water. Flying clouds, and cool. N.E.

MESSINA,

MESSINA, *March* 8.

THE Chevalier O'Hara, the Ruffian conful, who has refided here five years, has given us fuch a defcription of Sicily, that we by no means regret that we are about to leave it. The occafional remarks that I have made from time to time, are fufficient to fhew, that little of that comfort which we experience in England is felt here. Among the higher claffes, there is little domeftic happinefs, no hofpitality, and hardly fuch a thing as friendfhip known. External parade is what they chiefly regard, and the *principe* and *principeffa*, who place half a dozen laced footmen behind a gaudy carriage, live in dirty houfes, almoft unfurnifhed, and rarely receive friends or ftrangers to their tables. The fervants, though fine, are almoft without neceffaries.

The

The liveries are not their own, and they have but about seven-pence a day to provide themselves with meat, drink, linen, &c. This, at least, is the chevalier's account of the Messinese, but one of our countrymen, who lately spent some months at Palermo, speaks in high terms of the kindness and hospitality with which he was there received, and could we have prolonged our stay at that place, I doubt not but we should have experienced the truth of his assertion.

Beef, mutton, and veal, are hardly ever to be met with, except in Palermo, Catania, and Messina, and even there, are all but very indifferent. The pork indeed is now excellent, though it may be far otherwise in the heat of summer. We have also fine garden-stuff, but the chevalier is persuaded, that

that what they have in Ruffia is far better; " the heat (fays he, in fum-
" ming up his miferies) has killed my
" wife and two children, and there is
" not a bit of tea or butter to be had."
However, all the inhabitants of Meſ-
fina are not deficient in hofpitality, as we have this day had ample proof, by being invited by our banker, Signor Gregorio Faroe, to a very good and plentiful entertainment.

I went out in the evening to fee the laſt flouriſh of the carnival. The ſtreets were amazingly crowded, as there was a triumphal car, drawn by fix horfes parading through the ſtreets, and maſked figures within it, fcattering *bon-bons* or fugar plumbs among the people. The fame fpectacle was exhibited on Sunday, and having heard a curious defcription of it, I preffed on with the
mul-

multitude to fee the fhew. Juft as I was turning the corner of the ftreet where it was, I met a vaft croud of people, and one of the fervants, whofe office it was to clear the way, running after them with a drawn fword in his hand, with which he ftruck the firft he could reach, but I believe without hurting him. The enraged populace rufhed forward to avenge the infult, and a fcuffle enfued, during which, I was pufhed into an apothecary's fhop, and the door fhut upon me. The firft thing I faw, was two women all along upon the floor, that I had helped to knock down, but they got up without receiving any injury. I was foon re-leafed from my confinement, but do not know how the fcuffle ended, as I made the beft of my way home, heartily tired of mafquerading. Bright morn-

morning, fome clouds in the evening. Ther. 60.

March 9.

I HAVE great reafon to be thankful for the temporary imprifonment which I fuffered yefterday, as the mob immediately formed two parties, and the quarrel became fo ferious, that the man who began it lies dangeroufly ill of the wounds which he received.

We left Meffina this morning * in a little coafting veffel, called a fproronara,

---

* We much regretted leaving Sicily without vifiting the antiquities of Gergenti, whither we purpofed making our firft expedition from Palermo, but there fell fuch a great quantity of fnow and rain at that time, that the men who furnifhed us with litiga and mules diffuaded us

from

nara, which is nothing more than a six-oared boat, with a sail. We crossed over to Regio, fifteen miles, where we waited full half an hour in the street, guarded like criminals, till the governor came from mass, and gave us permission to walk about the town. It is supposed to have obtained its name from the Greek word ῥήγνυμι, *to break*, because *broken off* from Sicily by an earthquake, of which event the poet gives us an intimation in the following lines:

Hæc loca, vi quondam et vastâ convulsa ruinâ
(Tantum ævi longinqua valet mutare vetustas)
Dissiluisse ferunt: cum protinus utraque tellus
Una foret, venit medio vi Pontus, et undis
Hesperium Siculo latus abscidit: arvaque et urbes
Littore diductas angusto interluit æstu.

     Virg. Æn. iii. l. 214.

from it, telling us, that we had some deep clay marshes to go over, which, they feared, would be hardly passable;
so

We had at Regio, upon a smaller scale, the same melancholy view as at Messina: the mortality was less than in most of the neighbouring towns, as only one hundred and twenty persons were killed, of which seventeen were found dead in one house; several perished upon the sea shore, where the waves rose to the height of seventy palms, and threw the bodies into the air, which rested in falling upon the trees and ruins. The coast of Calabria is mountainous like Sicily, though, near Regio, there is a plain richly planted with oranges, lemons, figs, mulberries, vines, and some palm-trees, much finer than any I have seen in Sicily. The same kind of cultivation is continued up a narrow vale behind the town, in which is a

---

so we were obliged to lay aside our intention, and afterwards had no time, nor indeed resolution, when we knew the want of accommodations, to put it in execution.

curious labyrinth, compofed of orange and lemon trees, bending under the weight of a prodigious quantity of fruit, of the excellencies of which we can fpeak by experience, as they were prefented to us with the moft unbounded liberality, and afterwards a glafs of *liqueurs* to warm our ftomachs. The owner of the garden gains a fequin a year for every tree, except thofe of the labyrinth, which he never fuffers to be unloaded, though he might thereby increafe his income one thoufand ducats per annum. Thefe oranges are efteemed the beft in Europe, not excepting thofe of Malta.

The article of filk formerly afforded a very confiderable branch of commerce to Regio, but it is now almoft totally abolifhed by the weight of taxes impofed by the arbitrary government of Spain. The proprietors are first obliged to pay the king for the land, then for each tree, and then, when the silk is wrought, five carlins per pound. After all, they are not permitted to dispose of their merchandize any where but at Naples, of which the traders there fail not to take the greatest advantage.

We have been towed from Regio (twelve miles) by two oxen, against the wind and the current of Charybdis, which, though the terror of ancient mariners and the theme of poets *, on account of its great whirlpool, is

---

* Tum procul e fluctu Trinacria cernitur Etna:
Et gemitum ingentem Pelagi, pulsataque saxa
Audimus longe, fractasque ad littora voces;
Exultantque vada, atque æstu miscentur arenæ.
    Nimirum hæc ille Charybdis
Hos Helenus scopulos, hæc saxa horrenda canebat.

      VIRG. Æn. III. l. 554.

now no longer formidable, nothing appearing but a kind of ruffle on the water, and that ſo ſmall that little open boats are croſſing it every hour, in perfect ſafety; and indeed the very remembrance of that horrible vortex, which was once ſo dreaded for ſucking in ſhips, is now ſo totally obliterated in the neighbourhood of Scylla and Charybdis, that perhaps not one perſon in a thouſand of the preſent inhabitants has heard that any danger ever attended the navigation of the paſs or faro of Meſſina, as it is now called.

We have got ſomething better than Sicilian accommodation, viz. a tolerably clean room, with chairs and tables, but no beds, ſo that we muſt again have recourſe to our ſtraw mattreſſes. Overcaſt, and cold wind. N. W.

PALMI,

PALMI, *March* 10.

WE were towed twelve miles under the shore to Bagnara, and saw more of the effects of the earthquake, particularly near Scylla, where a large portion of a mountain was broken off and thrown into the sea; some of the new ground has been made into a vineyard, part of which, two years ago, slipt down with the plantation, and I think another part will soon follow. The town is in a singular situation, and said (with some propriety) to resemble an eagle, having an high rock for the head, two wings stretched out on each side a promontory, and a tail behind. Many of the houses escaped destruction, but great numbers of people were washed away by the sea, which flowed half a mile upon the shore, so that 1654 persons perished in this town.

Bagnara, situated on the side of a steep mountain, was entirely overthrown, and 4350 persons killed. It is rebuilding in a manner truly astonishing, when it is considered, that the ground on which it stands is subject to frequent agitations. As it was only ten o'clock * when we arrived at Bagnara,

---

* I have all along set down the hours according to the English method of calculation, but, throughout Sicily and Calabria, they regulate the time according to the setting of the sun, by counting the twenty-four hours round. Thus the first hour after sun set is always one o'clock, the second two o'clock, and so on to twenty-four. It has an odd sound to strangers, to hear the people talk of fourteen, fifteen o'clock, &c. and, till one is a little used to it, often causes much confusion; for instance, if in the month of February, you wanted to set off from any place about six or seven o'clock, according to the English way of reckoning time, and were not to accommodate your orders to the usage of the country, your beasts and litiga would be ready for you about midnight;

Bagnara, we endeavored to engage horses to carry us a few miles up the country, to see a lake which was formed by the junction of two mountains, but failing in this attempt, we desired our boatmen to put to sea again, which they refused to do, alledging, that it was too rough, and indeed it must be owned, that the waves broke in upon us so much, in getting our little vessel

night; and if you wished to have your dinner at two or three o'clock, you would have it about seven or eight at night. Besides, by this way of calculation, it is impossible the clocks should ever go right for a week together; for, as the hour of sun-setting varies, the clocks must be regulated accordingly. These inconveniences have been found so great, that, although in most parts of Italy they still number the hours round, yet in some of the principal cities, viz. at Turin and Florence, the clocks now go as in England, France, Spain, Germany, &c. and throughout the rest of Europe, for the mode of reckoning from sun-set to sun-set seems peculiar to Italy, Sicily, and Calabria. In others of the great Italian cities, the clocks go both ways, particularly in Rome and Naples, which oftentimes causes more mistakes than by counting the hours round.

on shore, that the boat had like to have been overset, and it was with no small difficulty, and with the assistance of fourteen or fifteen men, who, after many fruitless attempts, at length catched hold of a rope we threw out to them, that we were able to land. We now went in search of the inn, which was such a miserable, filthy hole, that we resolved to come hither, upon the information, that the distance was only six miles, and that we should find a *very good* inn at our journey's end. We hired a mule to carry a few necessaries (leaving the greater part of our cloaths to come the next morning in the boat), and set out on foot, without arms, trusting ourselves to the mercy of the Calabrian banditti, of whom we had heard the most dreadful accounts. We began our walk by ascending an high mountain, planted from top to bottom with

with vines, interfperfed with groves of young chefnuts, which are much cultivated in this country for the purpofe of making hoops for barrels. We were fhewn, by the way, a piece of rock that had fallen down, at the time of the earthquake, upon a man and mule, neither of which could afterwards be found.

The duke of Scylla, whofe palace at Bagnara was levelled with the ground, went upon the fea in a fmall boat, which was thrown up into the air, whirled round and round, and then engulphed with all the unfortunate perfons that it had contained. On the top of the hill is a fine champaign country, a view of higher hills covered with fnow, and planted to their fummits, and a noble reach of Sicily, the fea, and faro of Meffina, which fweeps like an immenfe river between the two fhores.

shores. We were then near the spot where seven houses were thrown down by an earthquake about two months ago, and had a perspective view of the lake, which we were desirous of visiting from Bagnara. The earth, for the space of two or three miles, seemed to be turned *topsy turvy*, which indeed was literally the case, and we were told that a man at work, with his oxen, was moved two miles without receiving any injury. Upon some parts of this hill the ground sounded hollow under our feet; a circumstance which was remarked in the streets of Messina during the great earthquakes in February 1783, and at no other time.

As a proof that all are not thieves and robbers in Calabria, in one of the most desolate parts of our walk, we were called back by a country fellow, to to pick up a great coat, which had dropt unnoticed, and which would otherwise have been loft. Upon defcending the mountain, we had a view of the fineft plain I have feen fince I left Naples, and Palmi at one end, encompaffed by woods of olives. Having fhared the fate of the neighboring towns, it is quite new, with an handfome fquare, and a fountain in the middle. Our *good inn.* Alas! alas! our beds are left behind. Cool and cloudy. Ther. at two in an elevated fituation, 53.

Palmi, *March* 11.

After many fruitlefs wifhes for a blanket in the various cold dwellings where it was my lot to fpend the night,

night, I at length obtained my heart's defire at this place, crept under one laſt night, and fancied myſelf very comfortable; but I ſoon found that this luxury was attended with a degree of pain as well as moſt others, as legions of fleas, ſtrong and powerful as thoſe at Syracuſe, ſoon iſſued out from their receſſes to feaſt upon me. This day we have been waiting the arrival of our veſſel, which is not yet come, ſo that we muſt ſpend another night in theſe miſerable quarters. So delightful a ſituation I have ſeldom ſeen, but here we cannot remain with any degree of comfort. Rain moſt of the day. Cool. 4220 periſhed here.

MONTE

MONTE LEONE, *March* 12.

HAVING obtained my own ſtraw-bed, a better mattraſs, and a clean covering, I ventured to yield laſt night to the preſſing inclinations to ſleep, which came upon me occaſionally, in ſpite of half a legion of my former company, and a ſharp cold air, which penetrated through all the cloaths I had upon me. About half paſt ſix we went to an high point near the town, from whence we could ſee Bagnara, and our provoking ſproronara at reſt upon the ſhore, though the morning was ſerene and fine. Longer in our dirty inn we would not ſtay, and therefore ſent our Italian back to the boatmen with orders to diſmiſs them, in caſe they could not come on in twenty-four hours to this place, whither we have travelled thir miles by land in an ex-

ceeding

ceeding good litiga, borne by excellent mules. By this means we have feen a very fine rich country, productive of great quantities of corn, large forefts of olives, fome fine oaks, and cork-trees of a prodigious fize. The ravages of the earthquake appeared on all fides, every town and village having been laid level with the ground, though they are now rebuilding in a fuperior ftyle to what they were before.

Here again we were promifed an inn good and *clean,* and as fully difappointed as at Palmi; having had very little reft for the laft three nights, I fhould have thought it a luxury even to repofe myfelf upon a chair or table; but every article of furniture had fo difgufting an appearance, that we turned back into the ftreet, really apprehenfive that we fhould be forced to join in chorus

chorus, " My lodging was on the cold
" ground." Happily, my brother fpied a
well dreſt young man among the crowd,
and immediately made him acquainted
with our diſtreſs. He ſeemed, indeed,
to commiſerate our caſe, but with a
too ſignificant ſhrug of the ſhoulders,
gave us to underſtand that to procure
us a lodging would be extremely difficult, if not impoſſible, moſt of the
houſes and convents having been either
thrown down, or ſo much damaged by
the great earthquake, as to be yet uninha-
bitable, and the people generally living in
barracks; however, our new kind friend,
after taking a vaſt deal of pains, has ſuc-
ceeded far beyond our expectations.

I obſerved in our road today an avenue
of remarkably fine old orange trees, not
very full of leaves, but covered all over
with fine fruit. Bright and cold. Ther.
at half paſt ſix, 46; at half paſt two, 55.

MONTE LEONE, *March* 13.

THE young man to whom my brother addressed himself last night, is son to the chief magistrate of the town, and has continued his civilities with the most unremitting attention *. We are lodged in the house of an ecclesiastic, who is a sailor six days in the week, and a priest one. He is also extremely obliging, and all the neighbors are swift as lightning to do us any service, so that we feel ourselves in a great measure repaid for all the difficulties we have lately undergone, by the cordial kindness of these good people.

* This hospitable gentleman shewed us his own ruined house, which had certainly been a very handsome structure, and much lamented that it was not in his power to receive us in it; but he and his wife now occupied a small barrack, which I verily believe he would have constrained us to accept, whatever inconveniences his own family might have suffered, if he had not found us another habitation. In what was called the inn it was impossible for a living creature to lie down, without being speedily covered with other *living creatures* innumerable.

A great deal of cotton grows in this neighborhood, large quantities of which we saw in the husks, expofed for fale in the principal ftreet of the town.

Our fervant arrived this morning with our baggage, having difmiffed the veffel, paying eighteen ounces (about nine guineas) inftead of twenty-eight, for which fum we were to have been taken to Naples. For greater expedition he travelled by night, and learnt by experience that the accounts of the Calabrian banditti were but too true. About eight o'clock, having juft paffed a fmall wooden bridge, in a folitary place, he was commanded to ftop, inftead of which he clapp'd fpurs to his horfe. He then heard another perfon cry out *amazzatelo, amazzatelo,* kill him, kill him. Upon this he thought it moft prudent to make no refiftance, but told

the

the robbers he had only two ounces, fomewhat lefs than one guinea, which he immediately gave them. After fome threats demanding more, and after having rifled a poor man who drove the baggage mule of fix carlines, (about three fhillings) they went off to fome of their comrades, who were waiting at a little diftance, fuffering our boxes to come on unfearched, as they faid money was their only object.

Left fome *confcientious* people fhould think it a meritorious act to murder us, we are obliged to make apologies wherever we turn cooks, for dreffing flefh meat in Lent, which I believe fome confider as the moft heinous of all fins. In many parts, they abftain even from cheefe, milk, and eggs, but in this town, a bull has been obtained from the pope to difpenfe with that
extraor-

extraordinary strictness. No one may presume to touch animal food, unless it be considered as absolutely necessary for his bodily health, and then he must have a written order signed by a physician. At Naples, where the people are less scrupulous, dispensations for the whole season are granted, to whoever chooses to purchase them, and the king receives the money arising from the sale. The price to the poor is only ten grains, or five-pence English; to the rich, twenty-five carlins, or about ten shillings English money.

As soon as we had dined, four of the chief men of the town came to visit us, and kept us in conversation above an hour; after them came two more, and then our civil friend and his brothers, with Signor Abbate, our host. The accounts our visitors have given us of the banditti of this country, afford an alarming confirmation of those we have received from other quarters, and which we now know too well, are by no means exaggerated. A man was murdered four days ago, in the same place where our servant was robbed, and that he did not share the same fate, seems to be a matter of much astonishment, to those who have been informed of the circumstances of the attack. We have taken the necessary precautions for the rest of our journey, and trust that through the blessing of the same good Providence, which hath hitherto so mercifully protected us, we shall safely escape from all those difficulties and dangers, to which we are constantly exposed.

The day before we arrived here, a shock of an earthquake was felt, and a few hours after we left Palmi, there was one there, so that we have hitherto been favored with a passage through this perilous country, without experiencing any of its most direful calamities.

Our civil friend, who is a man of sense and knowledge, has presented us with some complimentary verses, in French, composed upon our arrival, and signed Don Antonio Francesco Ribaldi.

Fourteen persons were killed here by the great earthquake. A sharp frost and ice last night *.

CAS-

---

* Uncommonly mild as all accounts from England state the winter to have been, so severe a season through all parts of the continent, where we have been, was scarcely ever felt. While we were in Germany, particularly when travelling through the Tyrol, the cold

CASSINO DI NICASTRO, *March* 14.

THE *Procaccio,* or king's carrier, from Naples to Regio, being about to leave Monte Leone this morning with two campieri, offered to take us under his protection, which offer we most readily embraced, so having presented our host with two ounces for our quarters, with ourselves, servants, muledrivers, and one other man, we sallied forth,

was intense, and all the way from Venice to Rome, we found the weather very little warmer; the month of January which at Naples is usually fine and genial, was for the most part cold, wet, and at best variable; and all the time we were in Sicily and Calabria, we had several raw bleak days with frost and snow occasionally; so that my brother, who was advised by his physician to spend the winter in a warm climate, frequently complained of being almost starved to death in pursuit of it; and when he was got into latitude thirty-seven, and found so little difference in the air from what it often is full fifteen degrees more to the north, he gave the matter up, and heartily wished himself by a good Shropshire coal-fire, being fully persuaded, that there was no country whatever where

forth, twelve in company, and flatter ourselves that such a gallant troop will appear too formidable for the robbers of Calabria.

For the first ten miles, we continued upon the same high ground on which Monte Leone is situated, and then descended to a fine plain, bounded on the left by the sea, and on every other side by lofty mountains. We

where all winter comforts were to be found more than at home. And indeed when we consider, that in Italy and further south, the great object in building their houses is to exclude heat, and that throughout Germany and Swisserland, you are either in danger of suffocation by the sickly unwholesome stench of chamber stoves, when they have been heated any time, or that you must shiver two or three hours before they can be made hot enough to diffuse any warmth through the rooms where they are, and that you never see the fire at all, I say when these things are attended to, I cannot help thinking that those who leave England, in quest of a warm birth to spend the winter, generally find disappointment, instead of the object of their wishes.

took a flight dinner by the way, upon the banks of a clear stream, in a grove of myrtles, intermixed with fine oaks.

Near the same spot stands a new house in ruins, which was thrown down before it was inhabited. The owner was so affected by this calamity, that he died of grief.

We had an agreeable ride in the afternoon, among large woods of olives, encompassing some small fields of green corn, which had an effect peculiarly pleasing, from the assemblage of the different shades. As we drew near the town, which is beautifully situated upon the declivity of a mountain, we fell in with a large party of peasants, returning home with their loaded asses, and nearly dressed in uniform. The distance from Monte Leone to Nicastro, is com-

computed at twenty-five miles, but I think they are very long ones.

We had two miles of rugged afcent, after our arrival at the town, which was reprefented to us as a neft of robbers and plunderers; we mounted this long fteep hill on foot, comforting ourfelves by the way, with the idea of repofing at eafe in this Caffino, to the owner of which we had a letter from the naval prieft of Monte Leone.

We had, however, the mortification of hearing, upon our arrival, that the houfe, which confifted of two fmall rooms, was occupied, but that an adjoining chapel was at our fervice, if we chofe to make ufe of it. Being no longer nice with refpect to lodging, we are thankful for any place that is fcreened from the air, and barred against

against the robbers, and really are now better off than usual, having procured a table to eat off, chairs to sit on, and having a clean floor for our straw beds, five of which, viz. three for ourselves, and two for our servants, we have disposed of in the most convenient manner we were able. My brother's is just before the altar, which is adorned with artificial flowers, and under a lamp which is continually burning before a picture of the Virgin Mary, to whom we shall be more indebted than any others who have paid their devotions to her in this chapel, if she grants us a good night's rest, and keeps us from alarms of the robbers below. I could wish the people had less curiosity, as they indulge themselves in peeping at us through a window, that communicates with the house. They must see our preparations for supper, and perhaps we shall

pass

pafs for Turks, when our fowls are brought out, as we did at Palmi. We have difcovered a little place where fome lime is kept near the chapel. Here we have made our fire, and fhall drefs our victuals. Ice at fun-rife. Cold. Th. 52. N. The oaks here are coming into leaf.

COZENSA, *March* 15.

I WAS fo thoroughly tired, that I fell afleep laft night in a few minutes, and never waked till I was fummoned at half paft three this morning, to purfue my journey.

Our little chapel proved a very comfortable bed-chamber. We all flept much

much better than ufual, having been quite unannoyed by vermin of every kind. We well rewarded our hoft (who had procured the key of the chapel, we fuppofe, from the prieft) for having allotted the confecrated walls to the charitable purpofe of receiving and lodging ftrangers; but when the prieft underftands that we were Englifh heretics, and that his fanctuary was defiled in lent by our eating broiled fowls in it, he may perhaps think that a mortal fin has been committed: however, as I doubt not but the holy man will have his portion out of what we gave, it may, probably, afford fome balm to his confcience to make amends for the profanation of his temple.

We continued to afcend for three or four miles, amidft very fine woods
of

of immense chesnuts and oaks *, and after passing over some snow, had a rapid and bad descent for a short way, through a large forest. Signor Procaccio was very communicative, and *entertained* us with a variety of stories, representing the perils and dangers he had encountered. " Just in *that* place " (says he) three years ago, I was " attacked by a gang of fourteen " robbers, and one of my guards shot " dead; just in *this* I had an encoun- " ter last September with six, three of

---

* One cannot behold these forests of majestic oaks, in thickness nearly equal to the mahogany-tree, and tall as the firs which grow on the Alps, without lamenting that it is absolutely impossible, in the present state of the country, to make them useful either for building ships or houses, from the extreme difficulty, or rather the impracticability of transporting them over the mountains to the sea-side, the use of wheels being unknown, and even the corn carried on mule's backs. Surely no true Briton can contemplate these hearts of oak, without exclaiming, Oh, what a treasure would here be to keep up old England's wooden walls!

" whom

" whom have fince been executed." Certainly no fituation can be more favorable for depredations of this kind, as the grounds are extremely wild and the woods of immenfe extent.

We continued our courfe for fome miles, amidft the moft magnificent fcenery imaginable, lamenting the unfavorable feafon for rural profpects; however, the concern we felt upon this occafion, was counterbalanced by the confideration of our greater fafety, as the country people who fubfift by plunder, live out of doors in the fummer-time, and rob or murder thofe who have not force fufficient to oppofe them.

Our mule-drivers have a fingular method of afcending the mountains, viz. by laying hold of the horfes tails, and suffering themselves to be pulled along with very little exertion of their own limbs. This method to me was more eligible than another which they also adopted, viz. of jumping up behind us, whenever they thought it convenient. We descended the mountain through a grove of chesnuts of astonishing magnitude, crossed a picturesque bridge thrown from rock to rock, and then mounted by a narrow dangerous path, to the place of refreshment, a little dirty town, and the first we have seen that has not been injured by the earthquake. We had ten miles farther to this place, through a country singularly beautiful and romantic. It consisted of a jumble of mountainous ground, thickly wooded and richly cultivated, almost covered over with small towns, villages, and cottages, placed in the most picturesque situations imaginable;

able; upon defcending to the town, we entered upon a fine carriage road, and faw before us an extenfive plain, encompaffed by rugged mountains, richly clothed with wood, and crowned on their fummits with fnow.

Being now arrived at the capital of the higher Calabria, and many miles nearer to the civilized world, it may well be fuppofed that we are got into comfortable lodgings, and are waiting for the preparation of fupper and beds, according to the ufual method; but alas! the change is from bad to worfe, for of all the filthy holes, called inns, we have yet met with, this is the moft abominable; however, there is no remedy, fo we muft be contented.

The peafants of this country wear yellow jackets with black trowfers and bufkins.

buſkins. The women have their gowns tied up in a knot behind, wide ſleeves, and the uſual Italian head-dreſs dropping elegantly down the back. Froſt and ice this morning at the Caſſino.

Morano, *March* 17.

Bad as Cozenſa was, we enjoyed one luxury there, to which we have long been ſtrangers, viz. a fire-place, about which we aſſembled to breakfaſt in the morning, but, before the concluſion of the meal, made a moſt unfortunate diſcovery; for beſides perceiving a moſt intolerable ſtench, in putting down our kettle it preſſed upon a ſoft ſubſtance that had long reſiſted the action of the fire, and which proved

proved to be a portion of human excrement that had been there depofited as in a common neceffary.

Cozenfa is a good fized town, but very indifferently built, excepting the convents, fome of which make a fine appearance. As we fet out yefterday morning, we faw a riding mafter exercifing his fcholars, and from the feats which they performed, it feems, that horfemanfhip is no lefs a fcience in Calabria than it is in England.

We continued our journey twenty-five miles, through a rich vale, which is rendered very unwholefome in fummer by the overflowings of a river, whofe fides are flat and marfhy. We were twice obliged to ford the waters, which were fo deep and rapid that a man walked on each fide the litiga to prevent

prevent us from being carried away. There are always a number of men waiting at the rivers, who tranfport foot travellers acrofs on their fhoulders; which, though a very dangerous operation, on account of the width and rapidity of thofe rivers, and the large loofe ftones which are in the water, yet thefe guides are fo expert and careful that feldom any mifchief enfues.

Two foldiers upon the road, who were travelling the fame way as ourfelves, offered us their fervices, which we did not think proper to refufe, notwithftanding we were already fo well defended. Indeed we had fome dangerous places to pafs, for thofe low grounds are totally uninhabited, and fo over-run with myrtles and other thick evergreens, that an ingenious robber might fpring upon a ftraggler quite
un-

unawares. The house where we lay last night is erected merely for the *accommodation* of travellers, and is such a curious tottering old structure, that the slightest shock of an earthquake would immediately level it with the ground. We preferred *this inn* to one four miles nearer Cozenfa, that had two days before been robbed by twelve ruffians, who stripped it of every thing, and used the woman who lived in it so ill, that she has ever since been confined to her bed by the bruises she received from them, though happily she is in no danger of death. One room where the meat was cooked, the bread baked, and where the fowls roosted, was for the greatest part of the evening, the only place we could find to sit in; and our company—mulemen, soldiers, a Neapolitan fiddler, and two poor young men, who kept the house, doomed to

speedy

speedy death by the effects of a Malaria fever *. As there was a great fire, but no chimney, the walls and roof were black as jet, and curiously adorned with cobwebs, furred by soot in a manner really beautiful. After all the inconveniences we had experienced, we were still too nice to submit to sleep in that apartment, and with that company, and therefore, without ceremony, searched the whole house for another chamber, and we found three, but the floor of one was so full of holes that there was danger of falling through; another was previously engaged by the pigs, one of

* This fever rages in the campagna of Rome, and in all the low grounds in the south of Italy, during the heat of summer, and usually terminates in a dropsy, from which the patient very rarely recovers. One night in such situations is fatal to a stranger, and it seldom happens that the natives themselves continue many months free from its attacks.

which,

which, that lay concealed under some dirty straw, jumped up suddenly and gave a great snort, just as my nephew was congratulating himself on the comfortable birth he had found out; the third room was a granary some inches deep in dust; we made choice of the last, swept away some of the filth, and sat down to supper, highly pleased with our discovery. As the musician was likely to keep fast in the strictest sense, we invited him to partake of our provision, which he eat with a very good appetite, and was so polite as to agree with us, that the church of Rome imposed too great a burden upon her members, in enjoining them *to abstain from meats which God had commanded to be eaten.* Morning bright and warm, with sirocco wind. Evening windy and cloudy. Th. at half past twelve, 63.

The first scene that presented itself upon entering the *black hole* this morning, was our company, arranged upon the floor in a very orderly manner, and all fast asleep (though several cocks that roosted over their heads were crowing amain almost inceffantly); some were wrapt up with a small quantity of additional clothes, and others without any thing, had fallen asleep with as much ease as a dog upon a stone floor.

We set out through a narrow vale, filled with low underwood, where our litiga-men seemed very apprehensive of robbers, and would not proceed unless the four guards kept close with us; they carried their guns ready to discharge, and looked so much like a cock-shooting party, that I could hardly persuade myself they had any other game in view.

We continued our route for several miles through woods, sometimes thick, and sometimes more open, with noble timber trees, baited at a neat house at the end of twelve miles, and then ascended considerably, over wild, diversified grounds, till we passed between two rocky hills into a sweet little vale, enclosed by snowy mountains. In this delightful situation we found Morano, a curious town upon the side of a steep round hill.

The prevailing color in this part of the country is red; eighteen men, who were at work together in a vineyard, were in exact uniform, with red waistcoats, and dark breeches and stockings. The women and children of the village are dressed in a singular manner. Their garments are red, bound with green. The hair is divided

vided before, according to the fashion of some modern bucks of the high *tibby*, and ornamented, or rather disfigured, by a strange thing stuck behind, which, for me, must ever remain a non-descript. Bright with hot gleams. Ther. at twelve, 60. The fine weather which we enjoy at present has brought the lizards out of their winter recesses. They are about eight inches long, of a brilliant green, spotted with gold, and the head of a fine burnished blue. The medicine called Venice Treacle is composed of the flesh of these animals, and others of the serpent kind, boiled to a jelly.

CASTEL LUCE, *March* 18.

OUR inn laſt night was, in compariſon of our uſual fare, capitally good. We had a fire-place adapted *to no other purpoſe*, and I lay in my clothes between ſheets, without being diſturbed by a ſingle flea.

More company joined us this morning, and the procaccio doubled his guard to conduct us ſafely through the moſt dangerous paſs in all Calabria. The whole party together amounted to twenty-ſeven. We aſcended by a very fine carriage road up an high mountain, near the region of ſnow which lay thickly on the top. We then came upon a plain, about three miles long, ſurrounded with higher craggs. The corn in this elevated ſituation is at leaſt ſix weeks later than that in the vale below; on the uncultivated parts are many purple crocuſes, cufes, of the fame kind as thofe that ornament our Englifh gardens.

Upon leaving this plain, we entered the terrific pafs. It is a deep chafm between towering mountains, darkened by the thickeft fhade, fo that a fmall party of robbers, by fecuring a good fituation on the higher parts, may begin an attack upon a large company without the leaft fear of being overcome, as they might eafily efcape among the thickets, fhould the travellers attempt to climb the rocks, and make them prifoners. We defcended by a very rugged path, which led us out of the chafm to a foreft of noble oaks, and then entering upon a fine new road, foon arrived at Rotunda, a little town fo called from its fingular fituation, being built upon a conical hill, detached from all others, and not unlike Glaftonbury Tor hill in Somerfetfhire. After

ter a little refreshment, we continued our journey along the same fine road through a most enchanting vale to this place, (twenty miles from Marona) where we seem to have got a tolerable inn.

We have now taken our leave of the two Calabria's, so famous for their desperate banditti, and surely the most savage country in Europe. Every traveller we met carried arms, and the very peasants walked in companies with guns upon their shoulders. A chevalier of Malta was murdered not long since upon the same road that we have passed over in safety, which occasioned a friend of his, who arrived at Messina while we were there, to engage no less than twelve guards to accompany him.

Our musical companion has given us such an unfavorable account of Sproronaras,

naras, that since it has pleased God to protect us by land, we do not regret having left ours at Bagnara. He was thirty-seven days going from Naples to a place thirteen miles on this side Cozensa, and was once so near a vessel manned by Algerine pirates, that they presented their musquets at him. Had it been our lot to have visited Africa, we should probably have experienced greater hardships than ever we did in Calabria. What *might* have happened, convinces me that the wise Disposer of *all* events has guarded our every step by his providential care, and has made us acquainted with the magnitude of our danger, that we may the more acknowledge his goodness in delivering us from it. We have been wonderfully supported during the whole journey, and even enjoyed a more than usual share of health. A mercy for which

we

we can never be sufficiently thankful.

This inn contains a very decent kitchen, tolerably well furnished with the implements of cookery. The fire-place is near the middle, constructed of bricks, of a square form, and elevated about a foot from the floor. A large quantity of fewel is now consuming upon it, yet there is no chimney, so that the room is almost constantly filled with smoke. Bright and calm. N. Ther. 62.

Casal Nuovo, *March* 19.

Good as our inn at Castel Luce appeared to be, I was once more almost devoured with fleas, from which I made my escape at three o'clock this morning.

After

After afcending another mountain, we came down to a vale as romantic and beautiful as any we have feen. At the upper end ftands Lauria, under rocks, covered with evergreen fhrubs. The town is divided into two parts by a bold projection of the hill, which has a caftle upon its higheft point; near the bafe iffues a copious ftream, which rufhes with great rapidity under the fragment of an old arch. We began again to afcend upon leaving Lauria, along a very ftrong path, and through woods of prodigious fine oaks. We noticed a fmall lake in a very elevated fituation, the bottom of which, as our conductors informed us, could never be found.

About two o'clock we reached a fmall town called Lago Nero, from whence the great carriage road is continued

tinued to Naples. The beſt, and indeed the only vehicle we have been able to procure here, is a two wheel'd chaiſe, drawn by a pair of mules, which never trot, but walk, at the rate of about four miles an hour. We have come ten miles through a fine wild country to a ſingle houſe, where we are likely to fare tolerably well.

From Lago Nero to the entrance into Naples is exactly ninety-eight miles, and about a hundred to the king's palace, during the whole of which the road is finer than can well be imagined, being not only broad and even, but carried through the mountains at an enormous expence. Wherever we met with any carriage road before this, it was only for a few miles, as far as a particular diſtrict extended, but it was all equally good, or if poſſible better, no wheels whatever having been upon it, though part of it has been made more than ten years; and till it be all joined, (which had it not been for the dreadful havock and depopulation made by the great earthquake about eight years ago, would probably have been the cafe before this time) no carriage can go over thofe parts, which are yet untouched to thofe that are finifhed; however, it is going on in different places with great fpirit and vigor. We faw not lefs than two or three hundred people at work with barrows, fpades, picks, bafkets, &c. the latter of which were chiefly carried by women and children, which are fo very numerous throughout Calabria, that it is no uncommon fight to fee from fifteen to twenty in one houfe, or about the door. And indeed when we confider that the women

men marry at twelve or thirteen years of age, and continue to breed as long as those in more northern climates, we cannot wonder at the great population we see in every part of this country, nor that it should so soon recover from the desolations made by earthquakes. Foggy till eight, then bright, calm and hot. Ther. on the mountain, 65.

March 20.

OUR accommodations now begin to improve, as new houses have been built by the side of the new road, the towns in general being too close to admit the passage of carriages: we have not yet, however, forsaken our straw, which is very convenient when there is little time for rest, as it saves the trouble of undressing and dressing. We rose

rose again a considerable time before day-break, and travelled twenty miles over an high plain between mountains, very well cultivated and very populous. I could see seven towns at one view, two of them pretty considerable, and all within a circle of twelve or fourteen miles. The plain terminates abruptly, in an almost perpendicular rock, where the road has been made with amazing labor. It is formed in a zigzag, and built up with high walls of a prodigious thickness. From thence a flat bridge, constructed after the manner of an aqueduct, with two rows of arches, crosses a roaring torrent, and forms a communication with another rock, which, for half a mile or more, was blown up with gunpowder. All the galley slaves were brought from Naples, to accomplish this surprizing work. At the foot of the hill a large spring

spring rushes with some fall out of a deep cavern, which, as we were informed, proceeds from a lake three miles off, upon the mountain.

We continued our course thro' a charming country, and arrived in good time at this place, another single house, in a very high situation. Here the customs of *civilized* Italy seem to begin, as the landlord has demanded an exorbitant price for his room, though he has nothing to offer us to eat, and with a shrug of the shoulders, lowered it to our pleasure, upon our threatening to go forward. There is something like a justice's meeting in the house, and a great number of people, who are come to give in their evidence, respecting a murder. Fine bright morning, heavy clouds from noon till night, and a deal of distant thunder. Ther. on the plain, 60.

SALERNO,

SALERNO, *March* 21.

I HAD suffered so much from vermin in Sicily and Calabria, that I durst not trust myself any more in a suspicious place, lest they should rush out from ambush, and seize upon me unawares; on which account, though the *rogue's* beds seemed pretty clean, I once again laid myself down upon straw, and comforting myself with the thoughts, that it would probably be the last time, slept profoundly till half past two, when I was rouzed to prepare the breakfast, which we constantly took previous to setting out.

We reached Evoli, a town twelve miles off, at an early hour, regaled ourselves with some milk and cheese, which we found on inquiry was the produce of buffaloes, many of which

ugly

ugly animals we saw feeding in the neighborhood: some of the cheese we bought to carry with us to England. After our repast we dismissed our two-wheeled carriage, and hired two calashes, or one horse chaises, to carry us sixteen miles over a plain to Pestum, an ancient Grecian city, where there are three Doric temples, built upon the same plan as that at Segesta, though the style of architecture be somewhat different. Two of them have the same number of pillars, and the third a few more. The most perfect seems to contain a temple within a temple, a kind of *sanctum sanctorum*, inclosed on the sides, but open at the ends. The pillars are all fluted. The interior ones consist of two stories, but only two of the upper ones are remaining. In the largest, a row of pillars seems to have gone down the middle. The walls of the town form

nearly

nearly a square; they are broad enough for two carriages to go a-breast, and still remain by places to the height of four or five feet. The gates are also to be seen, and three square towers, two in ruins, and one perfect. Some of the largest stones are very curious, not unlike a mass of petrified bones, as they are an assemblage of pipes, connected together by stony particles. They were probably taken out of some cavern, and I understand, there is a large one near the sea, from whence materials for the building of the city were collected. While I was walking upon the walls, I saw an enormous black viper, which I should suppose was not less than four feet in length, but as it fled upon my approach, I had a very imperfect view of it.

At this place we were agreeably furprized, by meeting two Englifh gentlemen, Mr. O Donnel, and Mr. Dalton, with whom, previous to this interview, we had not the pleafure of being acquainted. Upon enquiring of them if there was any news at Naples, Mr. Dalton informed us, " that great " apprehenfions were entertained re- " fpecting the fafety of Sir Richard " Hill, and his company, who were " fuppofed to have been taken by the " Algerines. Perhaps, (added he) you " can inform us if the account be " true." My brother fmiled, and affured them, " he was happy to afford " them at that moment, ocular demon- " ftration to the contrary." Having heard much of the banditti, they were completely armed to ftand on the defenfive, in cafe of an attack, even whilft they were viewing the temples, but

but they might have faved themfelves the trouble, and the apprehenfions, as there is no danger of this fort, from the time you are out of the higher Calabria, and indeed we had difmiffed our foldiers ever fince we left Lago Nero.

The firft part of the road from Evoli to Peftum, nearly as far as the ferry, is made very good for a carriage; there are, however, fome deep miry holes to pafs, as well as a few miles of clay ground, which are at leaft very difagreeable, on which account I would advife all who go from Naples to Peftum by land, to make choice of a dry feafon for that purpofe.

The inn at Peftum (though it appeared a palace to us) is a very bad one, and 'tis moft probable nothing to eat

eat can be had there. I would therefore advise all my countrymen, whose curiosity may excite them to visit these magnificent temples, to sleep the first night at Salerno, where there are two good inns, to set off very early next morning for Pestum, to carry some refreshment with them, to see the antiquities, (which will not take more than two hours to the most curious observer, during which time their horses will be baited at the *hosteria*, or public house,) and to return to Salerno at night.

In this way our kind friends beforementioned easily performed the journey in the month of March last, when they gave us every cause to remember as well as to be thankful for the rencontre, for they not only entertained us most hospitably at the Pestum inn with

an

an admirable piece of cold roaſt beef, which they carried with them from Naples, (a curioſity which we had not ſeen ſince our departure from that city) but preſented us with a bottle of excellent white hermitage, which Mr. O Donnel had brought from France.

We returned in our calaſhes to Evoli, from whence we have travelled like gentlemen another ſixteen miles, in a handſome coach, drawn by four excellent horſes to this place, and with no ſmall pleaſure anticipate the idea of having a comfortable meal, and repoſing ourſelves in ſome good beds, that are now preparing for us. The payment for our quarters, or according to the Sicilian phraſe, *per l'incommodo* (for the inconvenience we cauſed) has always been left to our generoſity, which I believe, generally exceeded all expectation,

tion, as the wretched poverty of the people commonly drew half a guinea or more, according to Englifh money, from our pockets. Future travellers may, perhaps, complain of our *fpoiling the inns*, but I am fure they would excufe us, if they knew the various fcenes of diftrefs we met with. One woman, who had many fmall children, declared with the warmeft expreffions of gratitude, that fhe had been prefented with a fortune, and would fain have kiffed my brother's hands, clothes, or feet, which is the frequent method of fhewing refpect. What is the common fum given upon thofe occafions, we difcovered from the generofity of our fellow-traveller, the mufician, who prefented the men of the *mal-aria* houfe with two grains, or an halfpenny, for his lodging, and a couple of eggs.

Laft

Last night, when we were got upon the new road, we perceived that Italian customs began to take place, as I have already observed, when speaking of the charge made by our *conscientious* host, though we brought our own supper with us, and dressed it ourselves.

We must, however, do our landlord here the justice to say, that he was not unreasonable in his demand, though, for fear of disputes, we thought it best to make our bargain for supper, beds, &c. as we had always done when we travelled in Italy. He told us his fixed price, *per i padroni*, or the masters, was fifteen carlins, (about six shillings of our money) per head, repast, lodging, wine, and every thing else, included. To this, we made no objection, and found our inn (Antonio, or as it was written over the sign " *Monsu Antonio*") clean,

clean, comfortable, and good. As I am on the subject of making bargains at inns, I must observe, that all throughout Italy, in going from one great town to another, we found it absolutely necessary, not only to make agreement, for our supper and lodging, but for fire, and a morsel of bread, and a raw egg in the morning, the yolk of which we used to beat up with cold water, by way of succedaneum for cream in our tea; whenever this was omitted, a dispute generally took place, and perhaps the value of two or three shillings more was insisted on, as the egg and bread for our tea were not taken into the *patto*, or compact.

But *a propos* of our tea-drinkings; at least, to say a little more concerning them, whether *a propos* or not, I have mentioned before that our tea was exceedingly

ceedingly useful to us, and that my brother esteemed it among his chiefest comforts in the eatable or drinkable way, is pretty evident from his asking our Italian servant, as soon as he found he was far more frightened than hurt by the robbers, "*whether the tea was safe,*" though indeed we had then but a small quantity left, having been quite too lavish of so great a treasure when Mr. Tough first made us the present at Palermo, upon the supposition that we should return to Naples some weeks sooner than we did. Our seasons, however, for regaling ourselves with this refreshing liquor, were very uncertain. If we found ourselves besieged by an army of nocturnal invaders, thirsting for our blood, we would pull off and shake our shirts, dress ourselves, boil our kettle, drink tea, and set off two or three hours sooner than we intended, in hopes of finding better quarters. Where we could get no beds, or only one among us, (as was the cafe before we had our own bags made to put ſtraw in) they whoſe turn it was to fit up, mended the fire, boiled the water, and made tea, an operation which at the houſe where the *deaf* man and his *bawling* wife lived, really continued the whole night. However, I here got ſome ſleep, and might have had more, had I not been prevented by my nephew's inceſſant burſts of laughter, and the ſickneſs of thoſe who had made too free with the ſweet wine.

And now more *a propos* of wine than of tea. The wines throughout Sicily and Calabria are for the moſt part bad and unwholeſome, being either ſweet or ſour, excepting ſome of the wine about Syracuſe, when it has been

long

long kept, which caufes much of the lufcious fweetnefs to go off, and gives it the flavour of a very fine rich madeira; but there is now very little of this wine to be got; malt liquor, brandy, rum, cyder, or cow's milk, there are none.

Salerno is an handfome town, built at the foot of a mountain, upon the fhore of a very fpacious bay, with a large fertile plain extending from it towards the fouth, but from the vapors arifing out of this rich flat, it is efteemed a very unhealthy place during great part of the year. Mild bright day.

NAPLES,

NAPLES, *March* 22:

In our road to this city we paffed through Vietri, which is a remarkably neat, pretty town, moft beautifully fituated about two or three miles nearer Naples than Salerno, but much more healthy and wholefome, efpecially in the fummer time, when on account of its height, and the refrefhing breezes from the fea, it is perhaps the moft agreeable and eligible place in all Italy for an Englifh family who feek retirement rather than company to fpend the hot months.

Though Pompeia, Portici, Herculaneum and Vefuvius were directly in our road, yet as we had vifited all thefe in former excurfions from this city, and as they are no part of Calabria, to which, and Sicily, it was my intention to confine thefe obfervations, and particularly

ticularly as so many more able pens
have been employed in describing these
places, I shall not intrude my remarks
on them upon the public, yet cannot
help adding a word by way of lamenting that so little progress is made in the
discoveries at Pompeia, especially as
there is an absolute certainty of immediately finding many curious and valuable pieces of antiquity, the search
having been put a stop to when the
workmen were employed in removing
the ashes and rubbish under which the
city was buried by the eruption of Vesuvius, out of a long, wide street, where
the houses and shops on each side remained almost entire, the paintings on
the walls quite fresh and beautiful, and
the marks of the carriage wheels, which
have worn away the pavement, as perfect as in the time when the city was
full of inhabitants, and in its pristine
glory.

glory. A few men are indeed at work near the entrance, but alas! the Neapolitan monarch has not sufficient taste for virtù and antiquities to prevail with him to have the busineſs set about with any degree of ſpirit and vigor.

During the time of our Sicilian tour, not many days after we had left Naples, there was a confiderable eruption of Veſuvius, but nothing equal to that in the preceding year: however, we were very ſorry to have loſt ſo magnificent a ſight; for though this mountain be but a child in compariſon of the gigantic Etna, and its ſtreams and pieces of lava but rivulets and mole-hills, when put in competition with the mighty torrents and mountains which flow from and are raiſed by the great Sicilian volcano, yet, in one reſpect, even what may be called a ſmall eruption

tion of Vesuvius exhibits an appearance beyond what Etna can ever boast, and that is by lighting up the city and bay of Naples, with the town of Portici and the opposite hills, covered with white houses, gardens, and vineyards, so as by night to form, perhaps, one of the grandest spectacles in the world.

I cannot conclude without once more expressing the gratitude we feel to that gracious Providence which has protected us thro' so many dangers, and restored us again to our former abode and comforts, which we now enjoy with peculiar satisfaction and delight. Much rain till past twelve o'clock, afterwards remarkably fine and genial *. Wind N. W. Our

---

* The reader may have remarked, that in my observations on the weather throughout this tour, I have seldom mentioned the wind being in the south, which Captain Chianchi told us it rarely was at this season of the year.

Our stay here, however, will now be short, having seen every thing worthy notice before we set out for Sicily: It is therefore our intention to return back to Rome, in order to be present at the celebration of the holy week, and for this purpose we have already written to our banker, the Marquis de Belloni, to procure us a lodging, though we are told there may be much difficulty in getting one, a prodigious concourse of strangers from all parts being already gone thither.

year. However, our Neapolitan musician (whom we left with the procaccio and soldiers) constantly fancied there was a change in the wind whenever he found one in himself; thus being pretty bulky, if he had made himself perspire copiously by descending from his beast, and tugging on foot up a steep hill, he cried out, *Scirocco, scirocco, fa gran' caldo; il vento e cambiato:* an exclamation which we heard the oftener, as the mule of this son of Orpheus having at least as much penetration as his rider, had the good sense to kick and wince with all his might whenever he found the gentleman going to remount, in order to ease himself of his burden as long as he could.

POSTSCRIPT.

THE ceremonies of the paſſion week, or as it is called at Rome *La Settimana Santa*, having been by far more brilliant the laſt year than uſual, on account of the pope having been honored by a viſit from the king and queen of Naples, and from the *Meſdames* of France, I flatter myſelf that the following extract from my journal during that period, including our excurſion to Tivoli, may not be unacceptable.

Rome, *April* 17, 1791.

THIS day (Palm Sunday) we went to the Sixtine chapel in the Vatican palace, where we saw the pope seated under a canopy, dressed in a robe of crimson sattin laced with gold. All the cardinals that were not confined by illness attended upon this occasion, and entered the chapel in great state, having their trains borne by their domestics. They then knelt down one by one, and kissed the sacred toe, while the robes of his holiness were held up by one of his attendants, after which they received from the pope's hands a branch of palm-tree, elegantly ornamented with straw-coloured ribbons. Others (I believe any body that chose it, who was in full dress) were admitted to the same honor, but instead of palm they were only

only prefented with olive branches, without any ribbons.

This ceremony being over, his holinefs was mounted in a magnificent chair, and carried in proceffion by twelve men, holding in his own hand the moft fplendid of all the branches, decorated like his chair, with crimfon and gold.

———————

Rome, *April* 19.

As no ceremonies took place yefterday, we went to fee Tivoli, eighteen miles eaftward of this city; all but the two laft miles are over the Campagna, which on account of its low fituation is fo fubject to the mal-aria, that the few inhabitants deftined to cultivate the foil

foil may be rather said to linger out than enjoy life.

The earth in places appears burnt, and sounds hollow; and there is in one part a considerable stream, so strongly impregnated with sulphureous particles, that the effluvia are carried by the wind to the distance of three or four hundred yards. The stench is hardly supportable, and the pungency little inferior to that of salts.

The town of Tivoli, once a place of great note, but now inconsiderable, is beautifully situated upon the side of the Apennine hills. It is famous for one of the finest cascades in Europe, different views of which have been taken by most of the landscape painters in Italy. The Tiverone, called by Horace Anio, of which it is composed, and which is about the size of the Avon at Bath, first takes one moderate leap about twenty feet, and thence a few yards farther precipitates itself under the arch of a bridge with great rapidity among broken rocks, which close by degrees, and conceal it from view, till it foams again into sight from under a great natural vault, called Neptune's cave. It there finds a small shelf, or ledge, from whence it falls again as high as the first time. The magnificence of the scenery is at this place increased by a collateral stream, which tumbles from an high perpendicular rock. These two currents, thus joined, shortly fall again; and once more after that, force their way through a vast stony mass, which lies across their channel. This little sequestered spot, amidst the roar of so many cascades, and so closely embraced by rocks and mountains,

mountains, is surely the highest treat that a lover of romantic prospects can enjoy. There are indeed few large trees to ornament the scene, but a variety of shrubs, and some vineyards.

The flower-de-luce, both white and purple, grows here in great quantities; and there is also a beautiful pale red flower, in all respects similar to the medea, except its color.

On the top of one of the hills are the remains of an ancient temple, commonly called the Temple of the Sibyl, but some suppose, from its being of a round form, emblematical of the figure of the earth, that it was dedicated to Vesta. It was originally encompassed by eighteen fluted pillars of the Corinthian order, six of which are still remaining. The interior diameter is twenty-

twenty-two feet. It stands in a court behind the inn, where is one of the best situations for viewing the cascade. Another small temple was erected near it, but the remains are now very trifling.

Some of the rocks are waved and indented in a very curious and beautiful manner, and were probably composed by the spray of the cascade, which carried with it minute particles of sand, and in process of time deposited a sufficient number to form a solid mass. I can upon no other principle account for the petrification of a carriage wheel which took place on this spot. The wheel itself, indeed, exists no more, but the incrustations formed round the spokes, the circumference and the nave, correspond so exactly to the respective parts, that no doubt

doubt can be entertained, that a real wheel was once inclosed within them. After all, I muſt own that I am not quite ſatisfied with this explanation of the caſe, as other rocks, at leaſt a mile diſtant from the caſcade, appear to be compoſed after the ſame manner, though there be not at preſent any water near them; they are, however, upon the declivity of the hill, and might formerly have been waſhed, by one of the collateral branches of the Anio.

In a vineyard near the town, are the remains of Mæcenas's grand villa, conſiſting of three rows of arches on the edge of a precipice; a fine ſtream now runs through them, and ſoon joins others that tumble down the ſteep rocks in various parts. The extent of this villa affords a ſufficient proof, that Horace

race never paid too great a compliment to the dignity of his patron, whatever he might do to his merit. One pillar of a temple of Bacchus, is shewn near the entrance of the vineyard.

Upon leaving this classic ground, we took a walk in a very formal garden, belonging to the duke of Modena, who has a large old palace at Tivoli, which, though delightfully situated, is at present uninhabited, and much out of repair.

Such was our entertainment yesterday; we suffered much from the heat of a Roman April, but having a comfortable inn at the Sybil, were sufficiently refreshed to see the remaining curiosities of Tivoli, and its environs this morning.

We set out upon asses, and after an agreeable ride of two miles, came in view

view of a waterfall, which becaufe lefs than the great torrent at Tivoli, is called *cafcadella*. It confifts of a large fheet of water, which prefents itfelf to the eye through a grove of olives, and foon dividing, falls down a vaft broken precipice. About a quarter of a mile farther, are four more cafcades, tumbling down the fame hill, two of them indeed comparatively fmall, but in any other fituation, they would be confidered as extremely fine. Thefe, with the remains of Mæcenas's villa, on the brow of the hill above, have chiefly employed the brufh of the painter, and are confidered by many as the moft beautiful, but, if I may be allowed to turn connoiffeur upon the merits of a cafcade, I fhall pronounce the firft near the temple, the moft picturefque, fince that iffues from the bofom of the mountain, whilft thefe only fall from its fide.

We

We croffed the valley over an ancient confular bridge, again afcended by an old Roman road, and met our carriage at a fmall round temple, dedicated to the goddefs of COUGHING.

We next went to Adrian's villa, an immenfe pile of ruins, at the bottom of the hill, where moft of the beft antiquities preferved in the different mufeums at Rome have been difcovered. We were here fhewn the remains of two amphitheatres, part of the foldier's barracks, which confifted of an hundred chambers, all of the fame dimenfions, connected with each other, rooms for the flaves, with fome fragments of temples, befides a large inclofed hollow, once filled with water, and intended for boat-races. The remains of this magnificent palace, are all of brick, extremely maffy. The
royal

royal apartments were lined with ſtuccoe, and adorned with beautiful freſco paintings, ſome ſmall ſpecimens of which are ſtill preſerved, as alſo of the marble pillars which originally ſtood in thoſe chambers. While we were exploring theſe ruins, our Italian ſervant adviſed us to look under our feet, as he ſaid there was a ſtrong ſmell of ſerpents, which frequently lie in the long graſs that grows among the looſe ſtones; however, we ſaw none. Hot and ſultry. Diſtant thunder.

Rome, *April* 20.

The king and queen of Naples arrived this morning from Florence. In the afternoon, we went in full dreſs ſuits of mourning, in which only we could

could be admitted, to the fixtine chapel to hear the famous *miserere*. The principal part confisted in chanting pfalms, but at the beginning and conclufion was a fhort piece, in which the effect of the different voices combined together in the affettuofo ftyle, without the accompaniment of any inftrument, was wonderfully fine. This ceremony was defigned only for the cardinals, as his holinefs did not attend. Some clouds and warm. Ther. 69.

April 21.

THE ceremonies of this day began with grand mafs, in the fixtine chapel, at which the pope himfelf officiated, in prefence of the king and queen of Naples, and the mefdames of France, who

who had boxes erected on purpose for them on the outside of the rails, which are placed to prevent unsanctified feet from treading in that *holy of holies*, where none but consecrated persons are permitted to enter.

Almost the whole time of the mass, which lasted nearly two hours, different ecclesiastics were dressing and undressing the pope, changing the mitres he wore, and lifting up his PETTICOATS, under which appeared fine Morocco slippers and loose stockings or trowsers of white satin, richly embroidered with gold. In short his holiness, though a stout comely looking man for his age, being turned seventy-four, was so loaded with his different vestments, according to the different parts he was to perform, that I was apprehensive the good old successor of St. Peter,

Peter, would hardly be able to support the weight of his accoutrements, especially as the day was remarkably warm, and there was a prodigious croud all about him. The embracing and saluting all the cardinals round *, was not per-

---

* The operation of *public kissing*, makes up no small part of the devotion of Pope Pius the Sixth, who every day about two o'clock, goes with one or two attendants to St. Peter's church, in a white gown and red slippers, kneels before two or three different altars, and never fails to kiss with great fervency, the foot of a brazen figure, which was found in the Tibur, and is called a statue of that apostle, though from the drapery, which has the appearance of the toga, it is most probably that of a Roman consul. Be that as it may, the warmth of this infallible father is not damped by uncertainties, for he kisses and re-kisses the foot of this graven image, but retires a little backward several times, when he repeatedly bows down before it as low as the Persian when he worships the sun; then approaches it again, and in token of his submission, puts his head under the sole of the foot, which he can easily do, as the figure is seated in a chair elevated about five feet from the ground. Before it is honored by the holy kiss, one of the pope's attendants takes a cloth and carefully wipes it, and as soon as his holiness retires, several persons, who wait in the church on purpose, run with great eagerness to kiss the foot them-

perhaps the leaft fatiguing part of the bufinefs his holinefs had to go through.

As foon as the mafs was concluded, the Pope, arrayed in a robe of fcarlet † and gold, and covered with a mitre of gold thread, was carried in his chair of ftate to a balcony in the front of St. Peter's, from whence he gave his benediction to an immenfe multitude of

themfelves, and to catch the falute warm from the facred lip, infomuch that the brazen toe is almoft worn away by the frequency of thefe embraces.

† Whofoever views the pope and the whole confiftory of cardinals, all clothed in fcarlet, all having taken the vow of celibacy, (however rarely they may keep it) all affembled in the city, fituated on feven hills, all joining in the prohibition of flefh meat on certain days, all fitting in the temple of God, and exalting themfelves and their own authority fo highly, as to difpenfe in feveral inftances with the exprefs commandments of God: I fay, whofoever views, and attentively confiders only thefe few particulars, muft certainly be ftruck with the amazing fimilitude between the modern Romifh church, and the fcripture predictions concerning that corrupt power.

people, that waited in the area below to receive it. This business was conducted with much solemnity. A party of foot soldiers, being drawn up in a line before the church, formed an area for two parties of horse that made their appearance at the same moment from each colonade *, and marched with colors flying and drums and trumpets sounding to the centre, where they dismounted and fell upon their knees together, with the vast assembly that surrounded them, who remained profoundly silent for a few moments,

* These colonades are joined to the church, and being built in a semi-circular form, constitute a noble area in its front; they are three hundred and sixty eight feet long, and fifty-six wide, and supported by four rows of pillars of the Doric order, forty feet in height. The area is of an elliptic form, seven hundred and twenty-eight feet in breadth, and six hundred and six in length. In the centre is an obelisk of Egyptian granite, seventy-four feet in height, or, including the pedestal and the cross, one hundred and twenty-four, and on each side, two handsome fountains which play continually.

in full perfuasion that the blessing about to be given would be efficacious to their present and eternal felicity. The discharge of a cannon from the castle of St. Angelo was the signal; when those who were in the most distant parts of the city assumed the same attitude of devotion, and his holiness, with a grace and dignity peculiar to Pius the Sixth, waved his hand, and showered on the heads of the attending multitude those blessings which they so ardently expected.

In the next place, to convince the people that his heart was not set upon the pomps and vanities of this wicked world, the holy father washed the feet of twelve poor men of as many different nations, (though indeed they were all made perfectly clean before) and then kissed them, after which each one was

was prefented by a cardinal with a flower, and a piece of money. The fame men were afterwards conducted to a table elegantly fet out with artificial flowers and fweet-meats, and ferved by the pope and cardinals with a good dinner of excellent foles and other fifh.

In the afternoon was performed another *miferere*, and as foon as it began to grow dark, a large gilt crofs was fufpended in the middle of St. Peter's, and illuminated in a beautiful manner. During that time there were four proceffions of men and boys up the church, carrying crucifixes and torches, mafked with linen veils, having long loofe gowns, tied round the waift, and a cloak of a different color. Some had fandals, and fome were quite barefoot. I muft confefs that had I met thefe any where elfe, my heart would have palpitated

pitated with fear, as the idea their appearance immediately suggested to me, which was that of beings raised from an infernal world, was not at all correspondent with a christian festival. Being arrived at the upper end of the church, they knelt round the altar, which the priests were engaged in purifying, and had little brushes for the purpose, like powder-puffs; but what were the particulars of that operation, I was unable to discover, on account of the crowd. There was at the same time an exposition of some relics, which were held out from an high balcony inclosed in rich cases. These consisted of a piece of the *real* cross, the holy handkerchief, &c. &c.

Among the multitudes that flock to Rome at this season, are a prodigious number of pilgrims, many of whom have

have confessed this morning to a cardinal empowered to absolve from some sins, which a common priest is obliged to leave among the *casus reservati*, or reserved cases.

We went at night to the Palazzo Doria, in consequence of an invitation from the *principe*, to whom it belongs, to meet the king and queen of Naples. The apartments were splendidly illuminated, and contained about a thousand visitors of the first distinction in Rome. Their majesties did not arrive till past eleven, when they walked through the apartments, paying attention to all the company with great condescension and affability, and then took some refreshment in a private room, after which a profusion of ices, lemonades, and cakes were distributed by an army of of domestics*, and the whole concluded with a grand concert.

ROME, *March* 22.

THE pope's guards, who are stationed at the avenues leading to his palace, are dressed in the most strange, whimsical manner imaginable, viz. in a suit

---

* The next day the servants waited upon us to beg something for their attendance, a custom prevalent throughout Italy, if ever you set foot in their masters houses; even the attendants of the vice-roy of Sicily, who had more the appearance of gentlemen in waiting than of domestics, took care to remind us that a fee was customary; and at Catania and Syracuse we were quite pestered with a set of beggars in livery, *only* because we had letters of recommendation to their masters, and once or twice made use of their carriages, though we were never asked to eat or drink in their houses. One indeed thought proper to apply, because, *to oblige his master*, we conveyed a letter for him to Naples. At the convent of noble monks near Palermo, the butler who so liberally dealt about the wine, actually followed us into the court-yard, and there plainly asked us for the *bona mano*, or a present of money, which we gave him on the spot.

composed

compofed of broad ftripes, of blue, yellow, and red cloth, and in ftockings of blue and yellow. They have a buff belt hanging over one fhoulder, a cocked hat, with a white feather and a large laced band, to fhew that they belong to a fpiritual, or rather an ecclefiaftical prince, of whom the other parts of their attire, are in many refpects, characteriftic. Thofe, whofe office it is to keep order during the ceremonies, are covered with a fuit of armor and an helmet, and look juft like the old figures in the tower of London.

A third *miferere,* different from the former, was performed this evening in the ufual place, after which the pope and cardinals went into St. Peter's, to pay their adorations before the crofs, which was illuminated in the fame manner as yefterday.

A very

A very splendid fete is made this evening at the Palazzo Colonna, for the king and queen of Naples, and an invitation given to all the world, but my nephew not being very well, we decline accepting it. Warm and showery.

ROME, *March* 23.

THIS evening the outside of St. Peter's was brilliantly illuminated. The principal lines of the building were thickly set with lamps, and the dark parts being invisible, it appeared like the outlines of an immense drawing, sketched in gold. By an happy arrangement of the persons destined to illuminate, the appearance was changed in a moment from studs of gold to flaming stars. The pope came to the sight

fight in a ftate coach drawn by fix
white horfes. Immediately after, there
was a very grand difplay of fire-works
from the caftle of St. Angelo, for which
his holinefs, out of compliment to his
royal guefts, gave four hundred crowns
extraordinary. The fudden difcharge
of cannons and crackers caufed two carriages to be run away with, by which
means two perfons were killed, and
feven others much hurt *. Warm and
fhowery.

THIS

---

* Grand as the exhibition of fire-works at the Caftello
de St. Angelo was, I think it little exceeded what we faw
at Loretto, when the miracle of what is called in the
popifh calendar *la tranflazzione della fanta cafa*, or the
tranfportation of the holy houfe, was celebrated on the
ninth and tenth days of December laft year. I fhall,
therefore, beg leave in this place, firft, to introduce an
account of the miracle itfelf, as it ftands (in fubftance)
graven on a plate upon the wall of the cathedral at Loretto, in old Englifh fpelling, though how it comes to be
recorded in that language is to me a myftery; fecondly,

give

March 24.

THIS morning the pope performed grand mafs at St. Peter's with the ufual ftate, and afterwards gave his benediction to a larger multitude of people than

give as fhort a defcription as poffible of the commemoration of that grand event. Firft, then, for the miracle itfelf.

When the Turks firft got poffeffion of the holy land, this houfe, we are told, was carried by angels into Dalmatia, but the people there, not paying it proper refpect, it only ftaid with them four or five years, before the angels took it up a fecond time, carried it by night acrofs the Adriatic, and dropt it where it now ftands at Loretto. Here it remained about a century, the miracle unknown, the houfe unnoticed, till fome holy man had a dream revealing to him the wonderful tranfaction, which happened, as the dreamer afferted, between three and four o'clock in the morning of the tenth of December, juft 490 years ago. He told his dream to fome more holy men, and thefe to others as holy as themfelves, till at laft it reached the ears of the holieft of all men, his holinefs himfelf, who ordered, or at leaft gave his *fiat*, for the building of a moft magnificent church, as alfo a fuperb cafe of white marble, ornamented in the Corinthian ftyle, to be erected

than attended on Thurſday; he then proceeded to the canonization of a female French ſaint, who had (as his holineſs declared with great gravity) performed *three notable miracles.* She had been dead an hundred years, for, accord-

erected round this little old fabric (where a prieſt ſhewed us the window through which the angel Gabriel fled, the fire-place at which the virgin warmed herſelf, the gown ſhe wore, and the cup ſhe drank out of), ſo that if the angels ſhould ever attempt to move it again, a very extraordinary degree of force would be needful to accompliſh the buſineſs. However, if want of reſpect in Dalmatia ſent it to Loretto, there is no danger of its ever going any farther, ſince it is impoſſible it ſhould have higher honors paid it, even in Rome itſelf, as what follows will no doubt fully evince.

A vaſt multitude was aſſembled from all parts early in the day. In the evening the biſhop, the canons, and all the eccleſiaſtics belonging to the cathedral aſſembled there, moſt gorgeouſly arrayed in veſtments of flowered ſilk richly and ſuperbly embroidered with gold. The muſic and voices on this occaſion were collected from Rome and every part of the pope's dominions. All the perſons of rank and diſtinction appeared full dreſſed, or as it is called in Italy, *in gala.*

When

according to the rules of the church, no perſons can be canonized till ſo long a time after their deceaſe.

In the afternoon, about ſun-ſet, there was an horſe-race in the Corſo, which is

When this moſt ſplendid exhibition was ended, the company repaired to the palace of the archbiſhop, before which the fire-works were let off from a vaſt machine erected in front of the church, and for beauty and variety they were hardly, if at all, inferior to thoſe of the holy week at Rome. Between ten and eleven, the devotion, or rather the madneſs of the people was raiſed to ſo high a pitch, that fire-works, crackers, &c. blazed and bounced, and cannons roared in every part of the town; but between the hours of three and four in the morning (the time when the *holy* man dreamed that the *holy* houſe was carried and fixed by the *holy* angels in its preſent *holy* ſituation) the cannonading was ſo inceſſant and ſo loud, that we felt our beds ſhake under us, and really trembled for ourſelves, as well as for the poor wretched old inn where we took up our abode; and obſerved, in the morning, that the floor and one of the beams of the cieling had actually given way two or three inches. We were told that the next day's fire-works were to exceed theſe, but we were thankful to eſcape in a whole ſkin: ſo we left Loretto and the *black lady*'s houſe, not leſs wondering

is the principal ftreet in the city, about a mile in length. The horfes were without riders, but made to go full fpeed by having little prickly balls attached to their backs, which acted the ftronger as the velocity of the poor beafts increafed. Seventeen ftarted, but one of them ran againft a carriage and died in a few minutes. The conqueror was prefented to the king of Naples, who fat with his queen in a balcony belonging to the Palazzo Doria. Eleven ftate coaches paraded the ftreet juft before the ftarting, and cannons were fired at the time, as if to

---

wondering at the gravity and demure looks of the bifhop and clergy, whilft they were keeping up the farce, than at the amazing folly of fo many kings, queens, emperors, and empreffes, (among whom the bigotted Mary of England cuts no mean figure) in fending fuch an immenfe profufion of gold, filver, and precious ftones (furpaffing all imagination) as there dazzles the eye, by way of devotional offerings to a parcel of mouldered bricks and an old black wooden idol.

an-

announce something of the greatest consequence.

The holy ceremonies concluded with a second illumination of St. Peter's, and another magnificent display of fire-works.

SIC TRANSIT GLORIA MUNDI.

FINIS.

Lately

www.ingramcontent.com/pod-product-compliance
Lightning Source LLC
Chambersburg PA
CBHW022110230426

43672CB00008B/1331